THE FUTURE OF
PROPHETIC CHRISTIANITY

Essays in Honor of
ROBERT McAFEE BROWN

Edited by
Denise Lardner Carmody
and John Tully Carmody

Photographs by
Peter Brown

ORBIS BOOKS

Maryknoll, New York 10545

Copyright © 1993 by Denise Lardner Carmody and John Tully Carmody

Published by Orbis Books, Maryknoll, NY 10545
Manufactured in the United States of America

Library of Congress Cataloging-in-Publication Data

The Future of prophetic Christianity : essays in honor of Robert
   McAfee Brown / edited by Denise Lardner Carmody and John Tully
Carmody.
        p.   cm.
   Includes bibliographical references.
   ISBN 0-88344-897-1 (pbk.)
   1. Theology. 2. Church and the world. I. Brown, Robert McAfee,
1920- . II. Carmody, Denise Lardner, 1935- . III. Carmody,
John, 1939- .
BR50.F83   1993
230 — dc20   93-117628
                                                     CIP

Contents

iii

Part III
VARIETIES OF PROPHETIC TEACHING

Preface

This little book carries a big charge of emotion. It is a *Festschrift* for Robert McAfee Brown, created by his friends and students, who present it to him with much love and gratitude. Bob only agreed to the appearance of this book on the condition that it not focus on himself or his own work but rather on what now strikes him as an urgent issue: the prophetic responsibilities of the Christian churches. While accepting this condition, we contributors have nonetheless hoped that by dealing with various aspects of such prophetic responsibilities, we might still pay proper homage to a man whose entire career has exemplified the vocation of a latter-day prophet.

With learning, grace, openness, charity, and, perhaps most winningly, lovely humor, Bob Brown has taught all whose lives he has touched how ecumenical and liberating the Word of God can be. So, it is a great pleasure for us to offer back to him a small token of appreciation, set in the genre about which he himself has taught us volumes: the provocative, one hopes prophetic, essay.

Bless you, Bob, as you have blessed us and myriad others. God bless you, Bob and Sydney, with many more years in which to remind us of all we can be, when we let our hearts keep saying yes to the creative dislocations of grace, no to the oppression of any of God's creatures.

In addition to what we owe our contributors and Bob Brown himself, we editors also owe thanks to Bob Gormley of Orbis Books for welcoming this project enthusiastically, to Robert Ellsberg and the staff at Orbis for carrying out the production, and to Betty Creech of the Religion Department at the University of Tulsa for excellent secretarial help.

Introduction

From his formative years as a student at Amherst and Union-Columbia, Robert McAfee Brown has felt the appeal of the biblical prophets. His doctoral dissertation and first book focused on *P.T. Forsyth: Prophet for Today*. His teaching at Union Theological Seminary, Stanford, Union again, and the Pacific School of Religion stressed a Christian theology called to make sense — justice and peace — here and now, as a blessing on its own age. Preaching, writing, and political witness, which have continued unabated in retirement, have merely varied this stress.

If a single model from the Hebrew Bible had to summarize Bob's vocational career, it would not be the Law (however estimable), or the Writings (however witty, in the ideal), but the Prophets. Nor would there be any dissonance when one moved to the Gospel. Indeed, it is easy to imagine Robert McAfee Brown most energized by listening to Jesus read in the synagogue in Nazareth:

> When he came to Nazareth, where he had been brought up, he went to the synagogue on the sabbath day, as was his custom. He stood up to read, and the scroll of the prophet Isaiah was given to him. He unrolled the scroll and found the place where it was written: "The Spirit of the Lord is upon me, because he has anointed me to bring good news to the poor. He has sent me to proclaim release to the captives and recovery of sight to the blind, to let the oppressed go free, and to proclaim the year of the Lord's favor." And he rolled up the scroll, gave it back to the attendant, and sat down. The eyes of all in the synagogue were fixed on him. Then he began to say to them, "Today this scripture has been fulfilled in your hearing." (Luke 4:16-21, NRSV)

The essays offered here in tribute to Bob Brown reflect on the challenges that biblical religion in the tradition of the Hebrew prophets and Jesus puts to the Christian churches today; on the resources that the churches can draw upon to respond to these challenges; and on what and how the churches ought to teach as they respond.

Concerning present-day challenges, our volume begins with an eloquent voice from South Africa. With passion, Allan Boesak, a prophet forged in the fires of apartheid, asks the churches to resist backing away from their properly political *Sitz im Leben* and not let their language be coopted by

1

secular politicians of dubious intention. Thomas Peterson follows with an
essay reminding all citizens in the United States and Canada with ears to
hear of the shameful treatment of Native Americans, past and present—a
treatment one can only imagine Amos or Jeremiah, Isaiah or Jesus, condemning roundly. Richard Cartwright Austin extends such an exercise in
painful anamnesis, focusing on how people in the United States have
abused the land—profaned the great gift of creation. Taking up the cause
of the subordinated sex, the regularly depreciated half of the human race,
Denise Lardner Carmody challenges the Christian churches to speak out
against the violations of women's bodies and spirits, for which any prophet
has to hold the world's religious traditions accountable in significant measure. Accepting this challenge, John Tully Carmody asks for a movement of
men that goes beyond breast-beating around the campfire to embrace the
nearly regulative concern of the biblical prophets for the widow and the
orphan—the most vulnerable portion of any society. To conclude this first
part, where the focus has been current challenges, William Sloane Coffin
calls for a truly internationalist, global vision, arguing well that only this
vision matches what biblical faith requires of us nowadays.

Intermediate between Part I, where readers may find a daunting bellyful
of challenges, and Part II, where they may find rich traditional resources
with which to nourish an adequate response, stand some arresting poems
of Dorothee Soelle. It is no accident that Soelle, one of our most moving
liberation theologians, should be a poet and a lover of music, nor that
several of her poems should focus on Bob and Sydney Brown, manifold
supporters of her prophetic person and work. The Bob Brown who marched
in the South for Martin Luther King, Jr., and with Abraham Joshua Heschel
against the war in Vietnam, is the selfsame who plays the cello and once
wrote for *The New Yorker*. The creative life is no enemy of the prophetic
life. The "life" celebrated in both phrases should glorify what Edward
Schillebeeckx has made the touchstone of all estimable ethics: the
humanum, Irenaeus's "human beings fully alive."

His concern for the humanum sharpened by living in Brazil, Richard
Shaull finds in the Reformed tradition resources of great prophetic power.
Were we to expose ourselves to them again, again let them take hold of
our imaginations and consciences, we might find our Protestant heritage
greatly quickened, once more sharpened to cut to joint and marrow. John
Coleman studies the Catholic sources of a prophetic imagination to much
the same end. From his study, the sophistication of the Catholic instinct to
participate fully in politics and culture emerges less as an occasion for
cynicism at church corruption than as an opportunity to contrast what is
not with what ought to be and emerge as passionate defenders of the
oppressed, eloquent champions of social justice. In midrashic voice, Elie
Wiesel treats us to probing questions about God and justice occasioned by
the story of Lot's wife, under the guiding conviction that "only if we remember the other can our own identity remain redeemable. . . . We are who we

are and what we are because of the other and our respect and compassion for the other."

When we regard the other, we can find ourselves to be oppressors as well as perhaps people ourselves oppressed. Karen Lebacqz's meditation on this situation leads to a resourceful probing of both pain and compassion that ought to show faithful readers what justice requires in their own souls. Writing from the welcome perspective of French-speaking Canada, Gregory Baum publicizes the pastoral letter issued by the Catholic bishops of Quebec for Labor Day (May 1) 1992. If we are inclined to think of statements by leaders of the institutional church as inevitably bland or overly balanced, this letter can be wonderfully disabusing. Perhaps a socialist Christianity is not an impossibility. Perhaps, indeed, it is how a prophetic Christianity is bound to ring. Janet R. Walton's essay on the prophetic challenges of our times to liturgists does nothing to alter this judgment. As she imagines a worship adequate to the praise of God and encouragement of God's people that we now require, it becomes clear that bread and wine carry little nourishment when we separate them from social justice.

Who better to bridge the way from this conclusion to the sort of teaching one associates with prophets—the manifold proclamation of the prophetic call for justice and right cult—than Saint Hereticus, a funny fellow sometimes confused, because of similarities in diction, with our honoree, Robert McAfee Brown. For this nonce, Hereticus has focused on Adam Smith and his *sequaces*—all who would make profit the great idol toward which to swing the censer. Deviating from this orthodoxy, Hereticus proposes a quite different "prophet motive," and in the course of elaborating its implications he cleans up much of the language sullied by the invisible hand of a Smithian free market.

Taking Robert McAfee Brown as a model, Mary Judith Dunbar begins our section on teaching with an essay indebted jointly to William Shakespeare and Jon Sobrino. Conjoined, the two show her a proper pathway to an academic excellence set in the service of justice and compassion. Also focusing on the academy, Jerry Irish uses several theses of Bob Brown to rethink how prophetic Christianity might shape liberal education. Our third prophetic pedagogue, Pia Moriarty, draws on Paulo Freire and considerable experience working with poor adults in northern California to illumine the deep learning that adult education requires, when we conceive it properly. Writing about the education that seminary students deserve nowadays, Bill Webber criss-crosses much the same ground, noting to nearly devastating effect the responsibilities any worthy prophet would lay on a seminary to engage with the poor of its own neighborhood. Leon Howell, editor of *Christianity and Crisis*, turns a similarly unsparing eye on American journalism. If one asks how the secular media tend to treat religion, one finds little to afflict the comfortable or comfort the afflicted, much to trouble the believer, especially the believer convinced that only the truth can set people free.

Our final essay is in the nature of a response — the first for the dialogue that we contributors hope to establish with our readers — to the preceding seventeen essays, nineteen contributions. Carter Heyward is an old hand at this kind of work, having done it for a *Festschrift* for Gustavo Gutiérrez, and in inviting her to take up this task, one can be sure that nothing properly prophetic will be stinted.

We editors are more than grateful to Linda W. Glenn for the annotated bibliography on the writings of Robert McAfee Brown that greatly enhances the scholarly utility of this volume. Begotten from the throes of a doctoral dissertation on Bob Brown as a theologian in the mode of a social activist, the bibliography covers all the books, major articles, and contributions to edited collections of studies — all the major places one needs to go, if one wants to track down the most crucial part of Bob's enormous literary output.

It is a special pleasure to note that the wonderful photos of Bob Brown at home come from the professional lens of his eldest son, Peter Brown.

Royalties from this volume go to the Robert McAfee Brown Scholarship Fund for Third World students at Pacific School of Religion.

PART I

CHALLENGES

The Church and a New World Order

South African Reflections

ALLAN BOESAK

The question of a "new world order" raises a number of issues, among which is the appropriation of the language of the church and the Bible by politicians and the challenge that that poses to Christians and the Christian church. I urge the church to try to understand what politicians are saying and doing, but also to understand what the church must now say and do in response. We may invoke the biblical image of the new world as created by God, the newness of the vision that the church is called to proclaim and share with the world, and the challenge to contrast that vision of the new world with the vision that politicians may have today of a new world. Specifically, I refer to President Bush and his talk of a new world order, and to President de Klerk in South Africa and his talk of creating a new South Africa, a cliché that has become a glib part of the political language in South Africa today. We must now ask how the churches in South Africa have been responding to the challenges that have come forward as the battle for the proper language of the nation has emerged.

Listen to what I am saying. I am saying that there is the language of the Bible, and there is the language of the politicians. I think we ought to be looking for whether out of this clash we can find a proper language for one new South African nation that needs to be born, one united nation, one reconciled nation that needs to come into being. Many people are well aware of the role that the churches have played, especially during the last decade. We church people were in the midst of the struggle, in the front lines of the struggle, without any shame, without any apology, knowing full well that that is the place where God speaks, knowing also full well that that is just about the only place for the church to be if we want to be the church.

Day after day, there was confrontation with the government. We became, in the words of Frank Chikane, "the church of the streets." We led our people out of the church services, out of the act of worship, the encounter with God, onto the streets, into the encounter with evil. We knew that those streets were dangerous streets, streets of battle and confrontation, and of fight, and of bleeding, and of death. We also knew simultaneously that as we led our people down those streets, we were leading them down paths of righteousness. As a church, then we actually read our Bibles and believed what we read, and knew what we read to be true. We were wide open then for the challenge and the inspiration of the Holy Spirit, and we listened because we knew that we heard the voice of God in the cries of anguish of the poor and the oppressed.

We saw the tears of Jesus in the tears of the children, and we saw the resurrection of our nation in the resurrection of our Lord and in the uprising of our children. We knew then that the *anastasia* of our Lord is also the uprising of our people to rid ourselves of this bondage and this slavery. And we knew then that God was not found in the cathedral, although we went to the cathedral to preach and to search and to pray, but in places of conflict, and on the streets, and in the gases emitted by the police cannons. In those days preaching was an event, not simply sharing words of common Christian wisdom. We knew that as we preached we were actually putting on the armor of God in order to do battle with the forces of evil. We had a vision of justice and of peace and of a human world, of a new world, but we shared that vision even while we had the courage to shape the vision of a whole nation. In those days the church in South Africa had the courage and the clarity of an unpaid prophet.

Then came February 1990, de Klerk's speech in which he announced that apartheid was going to go, certain laws were going to be scrapped, political organizations that were banned were going to be unbanned, exiles were allowed to return, and political prisoners were released. Later that month Nelson Mandela walked the streets of Cape Town and spoke to close to half a million people on the grand parade.

The reaction of the churches was a curious one. Immediately there were those who said, "This is really wonderful, because now the church no longer needs to play the role that it has played for so long." And a famous voice said the church can now return to being the church. Churches in South Africa immediately declared 1990 the start of a decade of evangelization. We talked about rediscovering the spiritual values of the church, placing within brackets the values that we lost while we fought battles in the streets with policemen and turned our church services into protest meetings. There were many who said, "At last now the church can speak with its own voice, because the political organizations are now free to speak for themselves. They must now take up those political responsibilities that the church has been forced to take up at a time of need: certainly it was not a natural thing for us to do. The roles can be reversed now."

There were those who were wondering what kind of role the church would now be playing. There were also those who were wondering whether the church had a role to play at all. Great confusion. Those of you who know me will realize that, theologically, hearing all of this, my very being rose up in rebellion. I cannot even begin to conceive of a church that now can "return to being the church." I say, "Wait a minute, what do you think we were then?" I have always believed that the battle against apartheid, the battle against the forces of evil, the engagement of the government at every level, was the very heart of our discipleship, not simply an attachment to it, not an addition to our discipleship ("we will also make this political witness"). No, our political witness was the very core of our obedience to God, of our adherence and allegiance to Jesus Christ as our Saviour.

Now, there was of course another element here. We were very proud of our achievement, some said, because at last the apartheid government was beginning to speak the language of the church. The churches could now say, and some of them are now saying, "Well, at last you see Caesar is beginning to understand the language of the church, and Caesar is beginning to speak the language of the church, and we should thank God, because this is a clear sign of our victory. God has been able to use us so wonderfully that even the politicians now know what to say and how to say it. They use words like 'reconciliation' and 'peace' and 'justice,' because these are now the food and drink of political dialogue both in South Africa and around the world, building new worlds, building new understanding, building new 'order.' (The church must also watch that. The Bible doesn't use the word *order*. Go and check it out. That's where they catch you, you see. *New world* is biblical, *new person* is biblical, *new man* is biblical, *new woman* is biblical. *New order* they slip in between. It's not there. It doesn't belong there.)

In this situation, all of a sudden we find for the church the word *harmony* is the new catchword. We've got to stop being so confrontational, they tell us. That time has passed. We have, I said last year, a new Constantinian period ahead of us. At best, they say, the role of the church now is to be the watchdog of society. I haven't heard a single church officially call, or continue to call, for a public apology from the government for what apartheid did to millions of people over so many years.

I have heard a call, not to the government but to the oppressed people, to "put the past behind us," to "be constructive in the building of a new South Africa," to "be forgiving." Now, if it is the duty of the church to call for forgiveness, it is just as much the duty of the church to call for repentance. You cannot call for forgiveness if you are not courageous enough to call for repentance.

What has happened? You will see that I am sketching a strange picture of the church in South Africa. I never thought five years ago I would speak like this. It is the truth, nonetheless. During the white referendum, in early March of 1992, it was curious to see the reaction of the churches. A few of the white English-speaking churches, traditionally anti-apartheid churches, called upon their white members to participate in the referendum and vote "yes" for Mr. de Klerk, without explaining that the referendum never should have taken place, without saying to their white members, "You should at least go to the polls with a contrite heart. You should get up on the morning of the 17th of March and you should say, 'God forgive me and, my fellow black Christians, forgive me that I am once again participating in an undemocratic racist exercise, making use of my white privilege and my white power to participate in a referendum from which you are excluded, in which you have no say, in which we have expropriated the right to decide for the future of all of this country's people.' "

I listened in vain for one church to get up and say, "The text that we must now preach about this morning, this Sunday before the referendum, comes from Jeremiah. In it God says, 'You are going into exile, into Babylon, but go and pray for the peace of that city, because that's where you are going to be, and in the peace of that city I will give you peace.' " I thought there should be one minister who would say to his white flock, "This is Babylon, this is exile, this is not what it should be. I go and vote because I hope that through my vote God will help to give peace to this land, so that through this peace somehow miraculously He will grant peace to this nation, but I do so with a heart that bleeds, and I ask God to forgive me that I must still do that." There were two people that actually told me that—Herbie Brandt of St. Stephen's Church and Charles Villa-Vicencio, my friend. But it hasn't happened.

You see, I'm using this as an example to show that something is wrong with our theological perception. Somewhere along the line we have forgotten a few things. What has happened? I don't rightly know. It might very well be that we have often in the church burdened ourselves with the wrong analysis of the situation. Some people are saying the church has taken the place of the liberation movement. When the movement was banned, the church had no choice but to fill the gap that was left. And so the church is only the last agent in a series of gap fillers, so to speak. When in the 1960s the ANC and the PAC and those organizations were banned, there was a void that was filled by the black consciousness movement. Toward the end of the 1970s, the black consciousness movement was banned, creating a void that was then filled by the United Democratic Front. Then early in the 1980s the United Democratic Front was banned. That gap was then filled by the churches, but there's no such thing as a stopgap prophet. That is wrong. What is the church listening to? What is the church seeing? Moments in history to fill gaps, and in those gaps to speak the word of God? Or is the church called constantly and in obedience to Jesus Christ to speak the word of God—not to fill gaps but to create gaps, to create a bridge and break down walls, so that the word of God can fill the space? Not to wait until somebody else says, "Oh, there's a little gap; let's run and let's do something there."

Maybe, secondly, we have had the wrong theology. Now this may surprise you, coming from the South African church, because you always thought that we had the right theology. I mean we were so great, we were all in the struggle, and you didn't know how it was possible that people could be so courageous and wonderful. And, yes, they were courageous.

I am simply now asking the question: Are we now confused about the role that the church is playing, because in our theology of struggle we allowed our theology to be dictated by the struggle, rather than by the demands of the gospel? So that now the people in the struggle are saying or suggesting to the church, "We are not so sure that you have a role to play." The church then steps aside and says, "Well, maybe we don't have a role to play." We're not assertive. We're not saying to Mr. de Klerk, "You have no right to tell the church which role it is that we have to play." We're not ready to tell Mr. Mandela, "You and your organization have no right to tell the church which role we have to play in the interpretation of that language."

We must constantly ourselves give the interpretation of biblical language. That's what preaching is for. We must continue to be partial in this struggle. We must continue the tradition of partiality of the God of Moses and Israel, who led them out of Egypt, the tradition of Jesus of Nazareth and the prophets, for the sake of the poor and the weak in our society. We must make sure that the change that they are talking about is fundamental; that is, it must affect the lives of those who are, as Jesus has said, the very least of my brothers and sisters. Any change that does not mean change in the lives of the poorest of the poor in South Africa is not acceptable change. I am clear about that.

And so, any change that leaves Crossroads intact or Tucosa intact or the Bantustans intact, or any change which still means that black people die of hunger while white people die of overeating, is not acceptable change. We've got to have fundamental change. We've got to watch keenly as a church (for we are the radical edge of politics) the compromises, the necessary compromises, made in the negotiating process. There's nothing wrong with compromise in itself. One has to do that. But if the compromise makes victims out of those already victimized for so long, then it's wrong. If the compromise is a comfortable accommodation of the ideas and the desires of those who sit around the table, and not an accommodation of the deepest needs of those who are not around the table, then it's wrong.

At the moment there is no other agency in South Africa watching out for this. The church isn't watching, either. Who is the loser? Those who have been losing for the last three centuries and more in my country. They are the losers. Key words for the church are not only democracy, but also justice; not only progress, but also humanity.

The church must say to the people, "Of course you must have the vote, but we must be honest with you and say to you that the vote alone is not enough." Political power without economic power leads to new injustices and new tyrannies. The church must speak on behalf of those who cannot speak and say it is wrong for South Africa to create a situation in which whites are quite willing to give up their political power as long as they retain their economic power and therefore retain the power over the continuation of the injustices, socially and economically. We must say to the people, "You must have economic power, because that is justice."

We must also say to the people, "You must not only have the vote, but you must find your voice." We are proud of our role. "The church in South Africa is the voice of the voiceless." That's okay for now, but it cannot remain. The church must work toward that point in our history where the voiceless will have found their voice, because it means that they have the right now to help shape the destiny of their country with dignity. We must address these issues plainly and honestly.

The church must challenge these assumptions around the whole question of white fears and black expectations, because somehow in the minds of people, especially in the minds of white people, if I read your newspapers correctly, the white fears are always coupled with black expectations because black expectations are so abnormal, so abnormally high. I have yet to go into conversation with one person from the western world who doesn't say to me, "Well, you know, how are you really going to address the most basic challenge that you face, and this is these high expectations of your people?" I would like to say that there is nothing abnormal about the expectations of black people in my country. I would also suggest to you that these expectations are fairly universal. What is it that black people expect? Good and honest government, people who rule over them with integrity, justice in society, justice in the courts, a home to live in that is a fairly decent place, decent education for our children, a job—what is so extraordinary about those expectations? Every single person reading this essay has these expectations. Why are our expectations all of a sudden too high, too unrealistic, too demanding? There's nothing wrong with those expectations.

Some speak of white fears as if that were the only reality. Even the ANC is guilty of that. Who worries about black fears? We are afraid, too, our people. We are afraid that white people would rather destroy the economy than give us equality. We are afraid that white people would rather destroy the country than live among us as equals and no longer as overprivileged white people. We are afraid that white people will somehow manage to create a new elite where the white elite at the moment take twenty percent of the blacks and then create a new nonracial elite, and the rest of our people remain just where they are and nobody will be any the wiser. South Africa will remain an unjust society. That's what we are afraid of. We are afraid of all those compromises that will keep the poor poor and the weak weak and will strengthen the hand of those who do injustice through power.

The church must address these realities. The politicians won't, because Mr. Mandela is afraid that if he does, white people in the world will say to him, "Oh, is that right?" He's not even worried about the poor white minority who have no future in South Africa. He's only worried about his own people. Now I told Mr. Mandela, "That's your problem. You take me into the ANC and that's one of the problems you're going to have, Father, because I'm going to say these things, because if it's right, it's right. It may not be the party line, but it's nonetheless the truth."

These are things that the church can only do if the church is indeed the radical edge of politics. And so there is no time for confusion. There is no time for hesitation. There is no time for vacillation, here or there or how. There certainly is no time for retreat into the safe haven of neutrality. There is no time for the creation of a safety net. There is no time for a cautious theology, because the theology of caution is poison to the church, and when that life in the church that gives it its voice to speak for God and for the people dies, the church may continue to live, but the people will die.

2

The Prophetic Challenge of Cherokee Artist Jimmie Durham

Colonialism and Dehumanizing Images
of Native Americans

THOMAS V. PETERSON

Among the many instances of injustice crying out for attention from the prophetic conscience of Christians is the plight of Native Americans. In the early encounters between Europeans and Native Americans, Christians either expected the indigenous peoples of North America to welcome them as saviors bearing the religious truth of salvation or they demonized them as worshipers of Satan to be destroyed. Few people have suffered more from such an ugly self-righteousness masquerading as Christianity than have Native Americans; few people therefore have a more compelling demand upon the conscience of Christians for prophetic justice.

The cross-cultural encounter between Europeans and Native Americans has taken place within the context of ongoing colonialism. The genocide and political oppression of the Indian nations of North America has been well documented by historians. Historians, for example, write about the theft of Cherokee land in Georgia and the Indians' forced exile in the 1830s from Tennessee along the "Trail of Tears" that led to the death of thousands of people. They write about Jeffrey Amherst, Commander-in-Chief of His Majesty's Forces in North America, conspiring with Colonial Bouquet in the 1660s to kill Senecas and other Indians indiscriminately "as vermin" by distributing smallpox-infected blankets. These crimes are barely acknowledged in high school textbooks and by the general public. Even worse, we pay little attention to the suffering of today's Indian peoples who still live as exiles on marginal land in America. We ignore the poisonous uranium tailings abandoned by the nuclear industry on Navajo land in the West. Statistical indices of poverty have led one Native American scholar to conclude that it would be better to be born in Bangladesh than on a reservation in North America, where the average life expectancy of males is 44 years.[1]

Our society not only continues to create conditions that condemn vast numbers of people to subhuman existence, but we also ignore and escape responsibility for our acts. How is this conspiracy of silence maintained in the face of historical facts and present reality? In part, control over the indigenous peoples of North America has been accomplished through images that portray Indians in stereotypical ways and by telling tales that mask reality. No one has done more to deconstruct these dehumanizing images than has Cherokee artist Jimmie Durham. Durham is not only a fine sculptor and conceptual artist, but he is also the author of several works on social criticism. He was an activist in the American Indian Movement in the 1970s. In 1975 he became the founding director of the United Nations International Indian Treaty Council (a consultative body), which gave Native Americans their first official voice on the international scene.[2]

One significant preoccupation in Durham's art since 1986 has been deconstructing the layers of false relationship that exist between Native American cultures and the dominant power structure of American society. Instead of presenting the vast array of his work that ranges from the visually stunning to the subtle text, I want to let one work, "Zeke Proctor's Letter" (1989), help us understand how our stereotyping of Native Americans is part and parcel of the colonial strategy of subjugating the indigenous peoples of North America. The four panels of this work are reproduced on pages 16 and 17 in this volume. Durham's original drawings are in color and contain much more detail and nuance than these black and white prints are able to show.

Assume for a moment that you are encountering this piece for the first time in an installation that contains other much more visually appealing work by Durham. The first question that is likely to arise in your mind is whether or not it is really worth spending so much time trying to decipher such a messy text. The drawings seem obscure at best and crude at worst. These panels are not the marvelous, finely crafted skulls or masks that lure us into appreciating Native American culture or, perhaps more truthfully, lull us into thinking that we can easily encounter Indians through their artifacts. Maybe we even salve our consciences about the destruction of indigenous cultures in America by preserving what our experts declare is worth preserving from those cultures that we are in the process of destroying. Even better, if we can resurrect some artist who appears to be creating beautiful artifacts out of the ashes of the destroyed civilizations, the destruction does not seem quite so bad. But Jimmie Durham doesn't seem to be cooperating!

Unless we have quickly passed by these panels by dismissing them as pretentious or silly, we are likely to be caught by the extraordinary irony of the English text in the first panel. We have noted some strange lettering

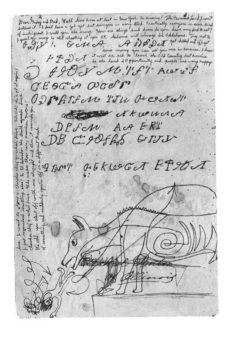 

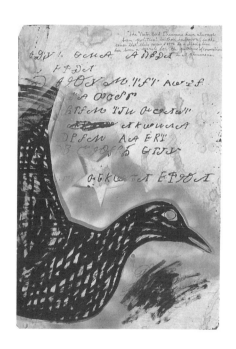
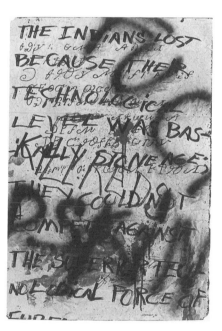

PHOTO CREDIT: FRED SCRUTON

that looks like a potent message from some archaic civilization, but have
no clue about deciphering it. Here is the English text from the first panel:

> Dear Mom and Dad, Well here I am at last in New York in America!
> The promised land. I can't believe it. I don't have a job yet but eve-
> ryone is very kind. Practically everyone is some kind of immigrant. I
> could join the army. How are things back home[?] do you have any
> food to eat? I guess the army is still shooting at you. OK lahoma will
> always be Oklahoma. Try not to get killed and if I get some money
> you can all join me in america. I know it will be sad to leave the old
> country but america is the land of opportunity and people are very
> happy here. I want to buy a Cherokee Chief 4-wheel drive. Whoa!
> He's at it again. I just remembered something else! In El Salvador
> the death squads drive Cherokee Chief 4-wheel drive. Who makes
> those cars; american motors? It's odd; you start off with one thought
> and then it reminds you of something and suddenly you're off on a
> different track.

Some of the ironic levels of the text are the fact that Cherokee country
isn't America; that the colonized Indians are asked to fight for their country
against people who are colonized in other parts of the world; that the
colonialists have even robbed the Indians of their name to sell vehicles that
are used by death squads. In opposition to our childhood images of maps
that show the 50 states encompassing all of the land in North America, we
are forced to consider that the Cherokees are a colonized people, whose
territory is not really a part of the United States. The contrast between the
"immigrant" who dreams of material wealth and the material condition of
the folks back home poignantly exposes the reality of life and death in
Indian country, even while suggesting the banality of our own commercial
dreams.

Well, now we're hooked. The seemingly crude and primitive text is
undercut by a sophisticated, acerbic humor that points directly to contradictions in the power relations between the dominant culture and colonized
indigenous peoples who only half-heartedly buy into the false promises of
a better life. Then perhaps we notice that each of the four panels is identical
in its replication of an archaic text that underlies the English words and
drawings. And we experience that something is completely inaccessible to
us. There is only a barely decipherable clue in the signature, "Ezekiel
Proctor of Illinois." We may discover that the underlying text is Cherokee,
whose syllabary was created by the Cherokee leader, Sequoyah, and that it
was the first written Indian language in North America. But at the same
time we become aware that much of Cherokee culture is inaccessible to us.

Even to begin to understand the Indians' alienation from American life
requires considerable effort, metaphorically analogous here to the effort to
read and think about the scribbled English text. There is certainly no short-

cut to Zeke Proctor's mind or quick way to understand Cherokee culture, even if we were to learn that Zeke Proctor was a Cherokee rebel who wrote a letter to a Cherokee chief to urge direct action against oppression. Contrary to our stereotypes that Indians had only rudimentary languages, we are prodded to realize that in killing and displacing Cherokees, we were destroying a people who had all the status marks of "civilization," including a written language.

And why is a coyote eating some poor fellow named Billy, possibly our immigrant to New York City? Coyote is, of course, the trickster in much of Native American mythology, and the trickster frequently gets his way through lying and making false promises. In the context of this first panel, Billy is someone who has been lured by American tricksterism to buy into the American dream and is about to be devoured by it. The trickster figure in this panel lends irony and ambiguity to the meaning, however. Sometimes the victims do, in fact, get justice; the trickster often ends up in a terrible mess caused by his own thoughtlessness and greed.

The second panel addresses the difficulty of being a Native American artist who resists having his art perceived as a marginal footnote to elite Western art. The English text, again overlaying Zeke Proctor's letter in Cherokee, states:

> There are sets of visual cliches in the artworld which are signs denoting sophistication. These visual style signs are unavailable for use by an American Indian artist who is from a different culture unless she produces bad copies which will be seen in art circles as derivative. To put the premise more simply, my graphic ideas and styles are kind of Goofy.

In the second panel the porpoise, a playful metaphor for creativity, is rendered in the style of Paul Klee. Here Western imperialism emerges under the guise of "high art" that is legitimized by the "visual cliches in the artworld." A careful examination of the panel shows some poor guy in the belly of a fish, perhaps Durham himself in the belly of the Western artworld, which separates "high art" from "folk art" and even defines authentic Indian art from the unauthentic.

Durham himself has experienced the difficulty of being an Indian artist in Western culture. He writes at one point, "I feel fairly sure that I could address the entire world if only I had a place to stand." But Indian artists are marginalized and treated seriously only if they create what Durham calls "Indian flavoured art."[3] In some earlier works Durham reconstructed animal skulls with skins, beads, feathers, turquoise, and seashells. Despite the fact that he saw his work as revitalizing animals that had been needlessly destroyed and discarded as valueless by our American culture, these beautiful sculptures all too easily permitted people to pigeonhole Durham's work into convenient and stereotypical categories. Rather than viewing these skulls as universalizing human experiences through a particular Cherokee vision of the world, people classified the skulls as "primitive" art because of visual clues of beads and feathers. Instead of paying homage to the animal spirits who were crying out against our civilization's callous acts of destruction, the skulls seemed to echo archaic images of a romantic past.

Durham, himself, now sees the skulls as "a show of bravado" demonstrating that "I could make art like any White guy, universal art. . . . It was supposed to be real art, it wasn't Indian art, it wasn't decorative art, it wasn't political art. It was from my place and nevertheless just as universal as their art."[4] Yet the skulls too often reinforced stereotypes of the "primitive" artist and too easily allowed Durham to be marginalized as an "Indian artist." Still, if Joseph Beuys and Anselm Kiefer can universalize German themes through art, why can't Native American artists universalize Cherokee or Navajo themes through art?[5] The answer lies in the way that we define authentic Indian art as existing only in the past.

A long-standing concern in Durham's work has been the misappropriation of Native American artifacts through museum displays. Some of his most humorous works are spoofs of archeological finds at White Plains, New York, of the Plane White People. An object called a "Muffler" is "reconstructed" with beads and feathers. An "archeologist" in a caption below the work speculates that "the muffler was a musical instrument . . . played in conjunction with the brake drum in the ritual Brake Dance, along the cane brakes of the Hudson River" by the Plane White People. Durham sees several obvious problems with Indian artifacts on display in museums: the museums' ownership of these artifacts is frequently suspect, since they were often obtained through theft; displaying masks, kachinas, and other religious artifacts amounts to sacrilege. But there are even more subtle issues. When Indian artifacts become displayed as objects of curiosity, the Native Americans begin losing their right to be subjects in a dialogue with other peoples. They are instead turned into the object of study and frequently relegated to a romantic past. Tragically, in the words of Durham, "There is an unspoken demand that we not exist as ourselves in this world, this terrible week, but exist only as nostalgic echoes of our ancestors—the 'real' Indians."[6]

The third panel of "Zeke Proctor's Letter" refers to the pan-Indian spirituality that has grown out of the Peyote cult. The image of the bird operates for the Peyote cult as the simple drawing of the fish did for the early Christians. The English message challenges the presumed distinction that European-Americans make between politics and spirituality:

> The Waterbird Dreamers have always been political in their endeavors; in the sense that their raison d'etre as a discipline has been a search for the patterns of connections of all phenomena.

Western notions of politics, inherited from the Enlightenment, assume that people are naturally contentious rather than cooperative. Both Hobbes and Locke, for example, assume that humans are essentially selfish by nature and that people have an instinctual desire for wealth and power. Government, in this view, must encourage compromise and must itself be restrained from becoming tyrannical through checks and balances. Governments must restrain human nature, even while limits are placed on the political order to keep it from becoming the tool of some interest group. At best mechanisms of compromise effectively prevent controversies from destroying society; at worst, political disputes evolve into warfare.

Durham is fundamentally challenging these Western conceptions by insisting that Native American politics is not viewed within a framework of conflict. Native Americans cannot separate politics from religion, because both are concerned with seeking the underlying harmony that is present in all life. Humans do not have to "sacrifice" their natural instincts, but fulfill their true nature when they discover their inherent interconnectedness with other people, with animals, and with the earth. Vine Deloria, Jr., a foremost Native American scholar, has argued that Indians had a very different conceptual understanding of treaty making than did officials of the United States Government. When Indian Nations willingly engaged in treaty making, they searched for an underlying harmony that could accommodate themselves and the white settlers, who had a very different life-style. When executed, treaties became part of a sacred obligation and were as much "religious texts" as they were political. European Americans, on the other hand, apparently saw treaties as a temporary compromise of fundamental conflicts that would continue to exist. Rather than binding sacred texts, they were political documents that would exist only until the next conflict required another treaty. Thus treaties did not ultimately prevent conflict but led to Native American bitterness along a trail of broken treaties.[7]

The very assumption that religion can be separated from the rest of life is a recent product of Western thought. Jonathan Z. Smith, an important historian of religion, warns scholars of the pitfalls in forgetting that religion as a category has "no independent existence" in the lives of most of the peoples that we study. "Religion," he writes, "is solely the creation of the scholar's study. It is created for the scholar's analytic purposes by his imaginative acts of comparison and generalization." It is a useful construct only insofar as the historian of religion is "relentlessly self-conscious" that the category of religion is part of the academic art. The study of any people's religion, then, must include a deep immersion into the whole culture and history of a people. Scholars of religion must be prepared "to articulate clearly why 'this' rather than 'that' was chosen as an exemplum."[8] Otherwise, academicians may drift into delegitimizing the cultures of living Native Americans.

On a popular level, the creation of "religion" as separate from life has allowed some non-Indians to portray themselves as Shamans. Writers such as Carlos Castenada, Michael Harner, and Lynn Andrews introduce themselves as the receptors of esoteric knowledge from Native American holy men and women. Whether their informants are entirely fabricated or have some existence in reality does not change the fact that the "Shamanism" portrayed bears little relationship to Native American spirituality, which places visions, rituals, spirits, drumming, and so forth solidly in the context of a community of people.

The spirituality of the Waterbird Dreamers always encompasses political, social, and economic issues. By isolating Native American spirituality from the life-style of Indian peoples, we can avoid guilt about abrogating the hunting and fishing treaty rights of Indians. Interestingly, after declaring Indian land in northern California important for Indians' "personal spiritual development," the Supreme Court allowed the U. S. Forest Service to build a marginal logging road through the sacred area, even though much evidence was presented that it would negatively affect the religious practices of three tribal groups.[9] When non-Indians claim that they have become Shamans, they help to delegitimize the spirituality of indigenous people who are continuing to struggle for their cultural self-determination in the name of a spirituality that is intimately linked to their everyday lives.

The fourth panel of "Zeke Proctor's Letter" directly confronts racism and hatred. It shows the relationship between a racist statement that is couched in an objective, scientific idiom and vicious hate graffiti that are obviously scrawled on the surface. The statement that masquerades as objectivity reads, "The Indians lost because their technological level was basically stone age. They could not compete against the superior technological force of Europeans."

We frequently encounter this type of social Darwinian statement, couched in language that suggests objective scientific thought. Durham here forces us to ponder how our statements about Indians that may seem innocuous on the surface give legitimacy to the vicious hate messages that seem to surprise us when they occur. In fact the graffiti can be countered more easily because they are more honestly direct. Indians are here shown to be doubly victimized. Not only have we destroyed their means for a self-sufficient life-style, but we also effectively keep them from integrating themselves into our society by propounding a racism that is frequently couched in scientific language.

The repetition of the underlying Cherokee text in this fourth panel ironically shows the shallowness of our glib statements about the demise of Indians and how these statements are made without any real knowledge of Native American cultures. It also clarifies that these statements are really about glorifying the civilization of European Americans and not about understanding Indians. This juxtaposition of texts challenges us to think about whether one could make an objective statement about the encounter between Europeans and Indians. My attempt at creating a text: "Indians were callously slaughtered by Europeans and their cultures were destroyed by a people who cared more for expropriating their land and resources than about encountering another people."

Through his art, Durham suggests that we non-Indians become brutally honest about the ongoing colonialism under which Native Americans exist. In the four panels of "Zeke Proctor's Letter," Durham helps us clarify how our political, artistic, religious, scientific, and racial views have been effectively destroying the indigenous peoples of North America.

Notes

1. Grant Foreman, *Indian Removal: The Emigration of the Five Civilized Tribes of Indians* (Norman, Ok., University of Oklahoma Press, 1932; reprint, 1953), pp. 229-314; Howard Peckham, *Pontiac and the Indian Uprising* (New York: Russell and Russell, 1947; reprint, 1970), pp. 226-28; Ward Churchill and Winona LaDuke, "Native North America: The Political Economy of Radioactive Waste," in *The State of Native America: Genocide, Colonization and Resistance,* ed. M. Annette Jaimes (Boston: South End Press, 1992), pp. 241-66. Note: This latter book contains essays of exceptional scholarly quality, documenting the situation of Indians in the United States from a variety of perspectives.

2. To begin exploring Durham's work, see his *Columbus Day: Poems, Drawings and Stories about American Indian Life and Death in the Nineteen-Seventies* (Albuquerque: West End Press, 1983). One of his few personal autobiographical statements is "Those Dead Guys for a Hundred Years," in *I Tell You Now,* ed. Brian Swann and Arnold Krupat (Lincoln, Neb.: University of Nebraska Press, 1987). A very important recent exhibition catalog is *Jimmie Durham: The Bishop's Moose and the Pinkerton Men* (New York: Exit Art, 1989).

3. Lucy R. Lippard, "Little Red Lies," in *The Bishop's Moose,* p. 24.

4. Luis Camnitzer, "Jimmie Durham: Dancing Serious Dances," in *The Bishop's Moose,* p. 9.

5. Durham discusses this issue extensively in his introductory essay "Ni' Go Tlunh A Doh Ka," (exhibition catalog with same title) Amelie A. Wallace Gallery (Old Westbury, N.Y.: Suny, 1986).

6. Ibid., p. 1.

7. Vine Deloria, Jr., *Custer Died for Your Sins: An Indian Manifesto* (London: Macmillan, 1969), ch. 2. Vine Deloria, Jr., "Indian and Non-Indian Conceptions of Treaty-Making in North America," address in a series of conferences entitled "Voices from Native North America" at Alfred University, Alfred, N.Y., 1990.

8. Jonathan Z. Smith, *Imagining Religion: From Babylon to Jonestown* (Chicago: University of Chicago Press, 1982), p. xi.

9. *Lyng v. Northwest Indian Cemetery Protective Asso.* 485 US439, 108 S Ct 1319. See also discussion of the case by Vine Deloria, Jr., "Trouble in High Places: Erosion of American Indian Rights to Religious Freedom in the United States," in Jaimes, *The State of Native America,* pp. 267-90.

3

Alienated from the Promised Land

RICHARD CARTWRIGHT AUSTIN

Bob Brown's theological gift is popularity. He is prophetic with good humor, profound without obscurity. He interprets others without taint of intellectual superiority. He offers radical judgment without belittling those he must criticize. He does not turn away any who hear him, but rather "gives light to the whole household" (Matthew 5:15).

We need such a spirit in the 1990s, for the United States of America begins this decade in a sour mood. This nation, "promised land" of the modern world, now seems less promising.

For many native tribes who hunted the woods and prairies of this continent before Europeans arrived, this was an abundant land where the skillful and the respectful could thrive in body and exult in spirit, communing with the great diversity of life that formed the beauty of this place. For most of the Europeans who poured out upon these shores during centuries of enthusiastic migration, this was a land of opportunity. America was, to be sure, a challenging place to begin life again, so much so that eager migrants were often fearful as they stepped ashore. Indeed when the Pilgrims first sighted their new world, William Bradford described it as a "hideous and desolate wilderness, full of wild beasts and wild men." Yet so long as there was land to settle and to cultivate, work for the willing, and the opportunity to shape social and political institutions, America remained a promised land worthy of risk and sacrifice.

Today there are still millions willing to wade to our shores, but it is the push of abject desperation that drives them from modern Mexico or Haiti, rather than the pull of a land with room for "huddled masses yearning to breathe free." Although America's countryside is depopulated, there does not appear to be land for the landless. Although our infrastructure of public facilities crumbles and thousands sleep in doorways for lack of housing, there does not appear to be work for willing hands. Although politicians seek our votes, they seem unable to respond to human needs.

America's natural beauty and vitality are slipping away, as well. Stately trees and rich minerals have been stripped from our mountains. Farmlands grow sterile beneath constant applications of pesticides. Streams discolor, and the life in them perishes below the discharges of cities and industries. The toxic refuse of modern civilization accumulates in poisonous mountains. Wildlife is depleted, species are endangered, and ecosystems are threatened. The very air we breathe, the source of life, is becoming a hazard to health. We have alienated ourselves from our promised land.

Often Christian churches have acquiesced in this alienation because our theology has been inadequate to inform human relationships with the community of created life. People of faith have lacked environmental ethics. The biblical image of "promised land" has been appropriated by Protestant bodies, in particular, to give religious meaning to the social anticipation at the heart of the American experience. But we have overlooked the moral ecology in relations with other species and living systems. American preachers have invoked "promised land" to inspire trust, hope, and thankfulness to God. We have not, however, recognized the moral claims of the land and the life upon it within this biblical image of a redeemed society.

In the Bible it is clear that land could be "promised" by God because God claimed, and retained, title to all land. "No land shall be sold outright, because the land is mine, and you are coming into it as aliens and settlers" (Leviticus 25:23, NEB). The creator who pronounced each creature "good" retains a primary interest in the landscape that all creatures require for their sustenance. When rebuking Job, God claimed the ecosystem, the web of life, as God's own dominion:

> Do you hunt game for the lioness,
> and feed her ravenous cubs? . . .
>
> Do you tell the antelope to calve
> or ease her when she is in labor? . . .
>
> Who unties the wild ass
> and lets him wander at will?[1]

God chose Canaan, the biblical Promised Land, to be the site for an experiment in the liberation of both people and nature from oppression. The descendants of Israel were enslaved in Egypt, while Canaanites themselves suffered beneath an oppressive feudal system. The Canaanite landscape and its living systems were debilitated beneath agricultural exploitation and scorched earth warfare. God determined that here both land and people would be rescued from power politics and brought into the lifegiving dynamic of moral relationships. They would become holy: a holy people, a holy land.

Under Joshua, land was redistributed in the name of God to every family that affirmed this covenant. A structure of moral relationships that embraced all creatures was articulated through sabbath law. Every seventh day, work must pause so draft animals and hired hands, wives and children, could rest. Every seventh year debts must be forgiven and indentured servants released, to slow the growth of the strong at the expense of the weak. Every seventh year the ground itself must be given rest and the freedom to grow fruit of its own choosing. Land could be used, but not enslaved. While at rest, the agricultural landscape—fields, vines, and fruit trees— must be available to poor people and to wild animals. Landowners could not be allowed to monopolize community resources, nor should agriculture be permitted to overwhelm its natural environment. At the Jubilee, seven-times-seven years, land reform was appointed, so descendants of the improvident and the unfortunate could make a fresh start, reunited with the earth.

The promised land was envisioned not simply as a just society but also as a healthy ecosystem, where no person, social class, or natural species would be allowed to overwhelm the interests of others. Prophets retained the conviction that the just distribution of land among people who would tend it with love would encourage natural vitality. By contrast, on the estates of oppressive landlords, the earth would withdraw its fertility:

> Woe to those who add house to house
> and join field to field
> until everywhere belongs to them
> and they are the sole inhabitants of the land.
> Yahweh Sabaoth has sworn this in my hearing,
> "Many houses shall be brought to ruin,
> great and fine, but left untenanted;
> ten acres of vineyard will yield only one barrel,
> ten bushels of seed will yield only one bushel."
> (Isaiah 5:8–10, JB)

This covenant vision, embracing all the life that the land sustained, was never fully realized. David won for Israel the peace necessary for the tribes to implement such a moral culture, but soon Solomon began the systematic subversion of tribal structures in the interest of imperial power. Solomon conscripted yeoman farmers to form the forced-labor gangs that clear-cut the cedars of Lebanon for timber to construct a new, imperial Jerusalem. Of course, Solomon included in his plan an impressive temple designed to appease God and the godly.

At a later age, prophets revived the ancient vision of land and people thriving together in a community of justice, and Nehemiah even imposed Jubilee upon reluctant landowners. Jesus, preaching at Nazareth in Galilee, announced a Jubilee to begin his ministry. This was a time to free those locked in debtors' prison and to restore just relationships between God's people and God's land. Jesus understood that a field of wildflowers was more beautiful than the robes of Solomon, and in his presence on the lake, even the fish crowded close. Although the spread of Christianity took it away from the Promised Land, Paul retained the expectation that, in the company of Christians, all creation might be liberated "to enjoy the same freedom and glory as the children of God" (Romans 8:21, JB).

From my farm in the southern Appalachians of Virginia, I contemplate the decline of the landscape and the sad fate of mountain people oppressed by the same forces that ravage the earth. Might different choices have been made along the way?

At the founding of the United States, Thomas Jefferson had a vision — almost biblical — of a nation of yeoman farmers whose contact with the earth, self-reliance, and participation in democratic society at the local level would assure the survival of freedom in this nation. Jefferson agreed with the biblical prophets that every family had a God-given right to land. He supported Virginia legislation to assure family rights to farmland, and he designed a pattern of homesteading for the Northwest Territories across the Ohio River that extended this pattern. The great Homestead Act of 1862, opening western lands to small-farm settlement, continued this tradition.

However, one of Jefferson's blind spots was his failure to recognize the value of the hunting and gathering cultures practiced by native tribes. While he was president, Jefferson treated the Cherokee chiefs of southern Appalachia with dignity and respect, but he urged the Cherokee Nation to settle down to farming, convinced this would benefit native peoples in exactly the same way it benefited white settlers. The Christian churches of the period, in their missionary enthusiasm, reinforced such cultural imperialism. The tragic result was that American culture lost potential contributions from native peoples who had the most intimate knowledge of our landscape — a knowledge at once practical, moral, and spiritual. This failure to value hunting-gathering cultures meant that wilderness preserves were not set aside for them and protected until, a century later, John Muir began a wilderness protection movement in the West. The opportunity for eastern wilderness preserving some of the original beauty and vitality of the Appalachians was lost. Most sadly, this failure of moral insight led, under President Andrew Jackson, to the "Trail of Tears" — the forced death march of Cherokee men, women, and children from southern Appalachia to Oklahoma. Other tribes were treated similarly.

Despite Jeffersonian laws to assure the spread of family farming, it was Alexander Hamilton's vision of a market-driven society that would more surely influence American development. When railroads spread across the countryside, farmers cut back on crops for local exchange to favor those that might be sold for cash and shipped to distant markets. Rural churches generally lacked the sophistication to critique market practices, nor did most congregations have the moral will to insist that godly people protect the community, practice neighborly assistance, and strengthen the disciplines of subsistence. Instead, when market commodity prices fluctuated from year to year, the homesteads of the weak were added to the acreage of the strong.

In the more isolated mountains of southern Appalachia, where I now live, subsistence farming continued into the early years of the twentieth century. Farmers cleared patches of cove and bottomland, grazed pigs on nuts in the rich hardwood forests, and felled selected trees to construct simple cabins or to float down the spring flood toward a distant sawmill. But when railroads penetrated into the mountains, speculators bought huge tracts of land and began the systematic cutting of the southern Appalachian forests. These were the most diverse and magnificent temperate hardwood forests in the world. It would have been possible to cut trees from these forests selectively so as to preserve their ancient character and to protect their future vitality. Indeed, modern techniques for sustained-yield forestry were first developed in the Biltmore forest near Asheville, North Carolina, but they were rarely applied. More common was the complete harvesting of all marketable timber from mountain slopes until, naked and exposed to the elements, hills bled their soil into the streams below.

Where coal was discovered in the mountains, mining companies also arrived with the railroads. Mountain farmers, little suspecting the wealth that lay beneath the ground, were induced to sell mineral rights for pennies an acre. Coal-camp settlements spread along the railroad tracks down the narrow, twisting mountain valleys, while mining shafts were cut into the hillside seams of coal. Again, it was possible to mine coal in ways that preserved human dignity and protected mountains and streams from pollution. Some coal communities were attractive and safe, particularly those owned by steel companies that shipped coal to their own furnaces, rather than selling in the fluctuating market. But the vast majority of companies were so oppressive that bloody contests ensued between miners fighting for decent wages, mine safety, and personal dignity, on the one hand, and companies that hired private police forces to assure the steady production of coal at low cost, on the other.

When I began ministry in the Appalachian coalfields in 1959, I found an industrial wasteland of streams choked with debris, burning gob piles of mine refuse, and idled mining families made redundant by advancing technology. Most of the huge underground mines had shut down, and in their place earth-moving equipment lifted mountain tops and cast them down the steep slopes toward the valleys below, removing farms and forests to expose seams of coal. Farm families that had surrendered mineral rights generations before now saw their homesteads invaded and despoiled, while mining families, displaced by the new machines, watched the hills they loved crumble before their eyes. So deep was the outrage that, when I pastored in West Virginia, we organized "Citizens to Abolish Strip Mining" and began a national struggle that eventually secured a Federal law for some measure of regulation.

Most people who remain in these mountains can no longer own land, for three-quarters of the territory is firmly in the hands of large absentee corporations. Mountain people now face a new indignity. Rather than beginning the process of reclamation that might in centuries heal the wounded landscape, many companies that have stripped the life and wealth from their holdings want to convert these properties to giant landfills for the debris from urban America. Mountaineers, threatened with further degradation of their landscape and further pollution of their streams with leachate from unidentified toxic chemicals, are again fighting back.

Our mountain story is distinctive, but we are not alone. Over the past forty years, people have been forced from lands all across the United States as the family farm system, Thomas Jefferson's pride, collapsed. In 1920 nearly 32 million Americans lived in farm families, and the majority of these families owned their own land. Today only 1 million Americans live on farmland they own. The largest group of farmers in America, over 3 million strong, are seasonal and migratory farm workers who have no hope of tending land of their own. It is not truly efficient to replace farmers with machines when, as a result, the descendants of farmers huddle in urban ghettos, unemployed and severed from their birthright. Industrialized farming is depleting rural communities and destroying the landscape, poisoning both earth and farm workers with toxic chemicals. Americans are now alienated from our own land.

We need a fresh moral vision of "community" that reunites humanity with nature in mutual sustenance, a vision that might inspire the political will to liberate both land and people from oppression. We need exodus from the fleshpots of market-dominated society. We need renewed covenant with the God whose earth this is, and renewed dedication to liberate our landscape and our people from industrial oppression.

Dominion is God's. Humans are entitled to share that dominion only if we tend and keep created life in ways that mirror God's love. We must never again imagine that humans have rights of exploitation over against nature, but we must envision, instead, relationships of mutual sustenance. To be fed, we must also feed, nursing back to vitality the lands that have been ravaged by industrial exploitation. When we struggle for human dignity and human rights, we must also recognize the dignities of other species, their rights to decent treatment, and their needs for sustenance from the domain God created for us all. Ecosystems must be protected along with human communities. We must invent new social orders within which people make peace with natural systems.

The spiritual resources for such renewal are all about us. They are in the Appalachian families that love the mountains and struggle to continue where their ancestors lived. They are in prairie farm families that hang on for the sake of their children, and in the migrant workers who dream of one day tending a few acres of their own. They are in the native peoples who keep the ancestral faith alive and who would again roam this land with love and spiritual discernment if given the opportunity. They are in the office worker who spends vacation time camped in the wilderness, seeking a bond with nature. They are in the ghetto child given a summer to romp on a rural farmstead. They are in our biblical tradition that announced God's promise of protection to every species emerging from the ark, survivors of the deep retribution that injustice precipitates. They are in our civil tradition that once offered every family a place to work or a piece of land to tend.

We need land reform: an orderly program, within our constitutional system, to acquire corporate lands and distribute them to any landless American who is willing, after appropriate training, to settle on land and tend it with care. We need to add to our Constitution new affirmations of civil rights for natural life that protect the survival of species and ecosystems, that guard places of distinctive beauty, and that direct humanity to treat all creatures with respect. We need to claim a new human right — in addition to life, liberty, and the pursuit of happiness — a right of access to nature, so no person is cut off from the natural world that God created. Every child needs a pet, a park, an opportunity for farm and wilderness experiences.

Churches must heal their anthropocentrism. They must affirm that the community God loved in creation and embraced in the covenant, the community that Jesus came to rescue from sin, oppression, and pollution, the community that praises together in the Psalms, is a community of all life. We must accept that "God so loved the *world* . . . " (John 3:16), and we must embrace God's creation within our worship and our ministries.

A century ago there were, all across America, communities of Christians experimenting with new forms of relationship to one another and to the earth: Shakers, the Amana Community, Mormons, and a host of others. Today the Amish and the Mennonites continue forms of sustainable agriculture that are at peace with the earth. I think there is no more important task for Christian denominations than to launch new communities that strive for healing and productive relationships with the earth. New public policy initiatives may be possible if we first build compelling demonstrations of how to repopulate America's landscape with families and crops, livestock and wildlife — healing the land within a community of life.

For five hundred years people of Christian, European heritage have colonized America, pushing aside native tribes, stripping off mountain trees and prairie sod, then even pushing farmers aside, all in a fervor to exploit America's great wealth. We did not discipline ourselves to learn how this land really lives. Now America's vital ecosystems are collapsing under the weight of modern society. We have alienated ourselves from our promised land.

Wes Jackson points out that, "The antidote to colonization is discovery.

We need to discover how the world works to know better our place in it. In this sense, the true discovery of America lies before us."[2]

Notes

1. Stephen Mitchell, *The Book of Job* (San Francisco: North Point Press, 1987), pp. 81-82.

2. Wes Jackson, *Altars of Unhewn Stone* (San Francisco: North Point Press, 1987), p. 27.

4

Christian Prophecy, Women, and the World Religions

DENISE LARDNER CARMODY

The prophetic mission enjoined on the Christian churches by the gospel of Christ includes calling their times to account for moral shortcomings. Whatever in secular society, or in the lives of the churches themselves, fails to match the demanding standard of love established by Jesus should come in for prudent condemnation. Does this prophetic charge cease when the churches encounter the ways that other, non-Christian world religions treat human beings? More pointedly, does the wholesale relegation of women to second-class status, if not physical and emotional abuse, that one finds in such religions fall outside the prophetic responsibility of the churches, perhaps in the name of ecumenical delicacy or the impossibility of judging a foreign religious culture?

The burden of my contribution here is to argue that it does not. With full awareness of the exquisite charity that Robert McAfee Brown would bring to an ecumenical consideration of a topic such as this, I propose that the churches fail their God and both halves of the human race when they do not speak out forcefully against genital mutilation, the burning of widows, female infanticide, compulsory veiling, and the great variety of other ways, both gross and subtle, that the world religions either abuse women or shunt them to the economic and social margins of the cultures that such religions inhabit. As well, throughout this brief essay I assume that the churches forfeit their existential prophetic platform when their own houses are not in order—when the sin of sexism disfigures their influence on the cultures they themselves inhabit.

Hinduism and Buddhism

The religions that arose historically in India have shaped billions of human beings in ways deeply inimical to a proper love of female human nature. The epitome of traditional Indian thought about women has been the conviction that no woman could achieve *moksha* (full liberation, human completion). Only men could achieve moksha, so women would have to be reborn in a future life as men. Certainly, there are myths of Indian goddesses that portray femininity as sacred, valuable, strong, positively mysterious, fearsome, and much more. No doubt, there are also myriad Indian households in which women are cherished as grandmothers, mothers, wives, aunts, sisters, and daughters.

But, there is also widespread abuse on the historical record of Indian treatment of women: subjugation to fathers, brothers, and sons; physical maltreatments such as beating, rape, and incest; murder (female infanticide, doing away with young brides once their dowry was received, forcing widows to mount the funeral pyres of their husbands); and a general representation of female human nature as less reliable than male, less honorable, by nature designed for submission and second-class status. As in virtually all other countries, in India, women have been poorer than men, more illiterate, more neglected by both civil and religious authorities.

Buddhism has taken originally Indian notions about enlightenment and freedom to East Asia, where they have interacted with Chinese, Japanese, Vietnamese, Cambodian, Thai, Korean, Burmese, and other cultural assumptions. By opening monastic life to women (tradition says that Gautama did this reluctantly, after much importuning by his aunt), Buddhists have given East Asian women a liberating alternative to arranged marriage. As well, some Buddhists have held that women are capable of enlightenment. Otherwise, Buddhists have done little to move social thought or institutions toward the acknowledgment that women are as human as men. Thus, by and large, one finds the female half of the population in all these East Asian cultures influenced by Buddhism still considered inferior to the male half when it comes to political or religious power.

Is it the place of Christians to criticize such historical, social, and religious biases? As long as Christians move humbly, with a full confession of their own record of sexism and their liability to misread foreign cultures, it is. One cannot bring the good news of Christ without causing a cultural ripple. The ideal cannot be to furrow nary an interlocutor's brow. The message of Christ, like the life of Christ, is a two-edged sword, cutting to joint and marrow. If the churches were convinced that women are as fully human as men, as fully graced by God, their analyses of non-Christian cultures would brim with critiques of the patriarchal abuses one finds in such cultures. Granted, one comes across such critiques from time to time. In my impression, however, overall the churches have been shamefully timid. No doubt in reflection of the generally shallow measure to which they have engaged traditionally non-Christian (in this case Hindu or Buddhist) cultures, they have not made themselves champions of female humanity.

I would agree with those who note the delicacy of a proper critique of non-Christian cultures on the basis of the Christian gospel. I would not agree with those who refuse to shoulder the burden of calling to account any abusive treatment of any portion of the human race in any cultural condition. I would say that such a refusal is a rejection of the prophetic charge ingredient in simple Christian faith — simple efforts to walk as Jesus did and reflect intimacy with God as Jesus did.

Confucianism and Taoism

Twenty-five-hundred years of Confucian thought have molded Chinese culture to misogynism. Among the principal relations structuring traditional Chinese thought, the subordination of women to men is second in influence only to the subordination of children to parents. Communist ideology made some dents in this Confucian legacy, but it failed miserably to demolish it. Indeed, the whole ethical structure of East Asia retains a Confucian bias against women. The main function of women is to produce sons. Whatever power women achieve is informal, won by their wit or bad temper. Social consensus grants them little clout. In fact, a suspicious gap between the number of female infants on the recent demographic books and the number that one would expect statistically suggests that female infants are still unwelcome in many households and so are killed. (This is also true in contemporary India.) If the Christian churches have engaged traditional Chinese, indeed traditional East Asian, culture sharply on this matter of misogynism, I have not heard any loud reverberations.

Taoist tradition can seem more favorable to women, inasmuch as many of the figures for the Tao are feminine. On the other hand, Taoism is a naturalist philosophy or religion, stemming from a pre-personal cultural epoch. Lao Tze and Chuang Tze are wonderful iconoclasts, but nothing in their literary legacy champions women as independent agents, free centers of consciousness equipped to criticize understandings of harmony with nature and within society that assume the subordination of women to men. The prophetic role for Christian admirers of Taoist poetry requires updating the legacy of Lao Tze and Chuang Tze without being anachronistic. One should not expect them to have gained feminist sensibilities over two thousand years before the rest of the civilized world. On the other hand, one also should not overlook the lacunae in their thought, if one wants to follow the evangelical Christ in championing the liberation of the poor, most of whom are female.

Judaism and Islam

Jewish women have traditionally suffered from both the biblical subjugation of women to men and the deficiencies of the Talmud. Despite the occasional vignette that depicts women as either strong or associated with good men in genuine love, the overall legislation of the Hebrew Bible comes close to considering women the property of men — chattel. Intercourse with women is incompatible with intimate dealings with God — one cannot follow Moses up Mount Sinai unless one has abstained from marital relations. The levitical priesthood works on this assumption, and the later laws about menstruation reflect taboos of millennial duration. All in all, Jewish women have been discouraged from studying Torah (the path to cultural honor), both because their proper province was thought to be the home rather than the shul and because their bodies have been considered more suspect than men's.

Islam has codified the second-class status of women on the basis of Qur'anic texts explicitly subjugating wives to their husbands. Traditional rights to a plurality of wives have further spotlighted the superiority of men to women. Women have been considered less reliable witnesses than men in court, and the rights of females in matters of inheritance have been less than those of males. If males would enter the Garden or be condemned to the Fire by the criterion of their obedience to Allah, popular Muslim thought has frequently held that females would enter the Garden or be condemned to the Fire by the criterion of their obedience to the men, fathers or husbands, ruling their households. Men have decreed that the dress of women ought to be, not what women themselves choose for convenience and beauty, but what would not disturb men sexually. Many African Muslims have accepted the non-Qur'anic practice of clitoridectomy, mutilating girls because it might control their sexual activity. So there is much in traditional Islam that a prophetic Christianity sensitive to the suffering of women would condemn.

The Christian churches only remain mute about these abuses of women at the price of forfeiting their prophetic license. In their dealings with Jews and Muslims, they only avoid concrete matters of ethical practice at the price of remaining superficial. Certainly, the implication of becoming specific, concrete, is opening one's own ethical practice to scrutiny by outsiders. Certainly, the huge blemishes on the Christian record are fair game for any Jews or Muslims possessed of feminist sensibilities. But this is what a mature ecumenical interaction among any of the world religions would desire: the frankest possible give and take; a measure of mutual respect, even mutual love, full enough to create the conditions for both strong accusation and deep repentance.

Reflections on Latin America

Along with Africa, where both Christians and Muslims face many cultural challenges when dealing with tribal traditions, Latin America presents the churches large problems regarding the treatment of women. Some of these problems stem from the influence of indigenous traditions, both Mesoamerican and South American, that exalt men over women. Probably more problems stem from the machismo brought by the Spanish and Portuguese invasions that began in the sixteenth and seventeenth centuries. The cultural mixture varies from country to country, but the Christianity that obtains in much of Latin America is no friend of women. Even when one admits the positive features in the cult of the Virgin, one has to call the Christian churches to criticize their own backwardness in both the defense of women's rights and the promotion of women's abilities. In radical, truly biblical perspective, women are either treated as well as men or the image of God ("male and female God created them") is marred, disfigured, crucified. The healthiest result of a courageous prophetic stance in dialogue with other world religions would be for the churches to criticize the cultures in their own heartlands. Few cultural malignancies in all the Americas are more glaring than the injustices afflicting women.

Reflections on North America

As Asian, Muslim, African, and other largely non-European, non-Christian cultural traditions spill into the lives of Canadians and people of the United States, prophetic Christians will sense a handsome opportunity to champion all the victims of injustice, especially the majority who are female. This is an immensely formidable, explosive issue, of course, because the status of women has been so central in most traditional cultures. The debate about "family values" that surfaced during the 1992 presidential campaign may have been largely bogus, but even so it reminded the astute that the possibility of women controlling their own destinies, rather than living as men desire, remains a truly incendiary prospect. How interesting it ought to be to church people, then, to consider the proposition that such a control could be women's birthright as disciples of Jesus.

Obviously, no human being accepting the gospel as God's best word can desire or propose a self-control that is fully autonomous. Obviously, the truly Christian view of human flourishing locates it in nearness to God, even mystical abandonment to God, because such a view realizes that we are made to commune with God, be divinized by the love that is God's being (as best our faulty minds can conceive it). God is always the potter, we always the pots. Nonetheless, when we talk about the cultural side of human autonomy, the freedom to which men and women can rightly aspire in their economic, political, religious, and other horizontal interactions, we fail the gospel if we do not grant women the same self-determination we grant men.

How vigorously do the Christian churches, as a collective body, defend and promote the cultural self-determination of women? Do the mainstream or liberal churches even try to offset, through their prophetic critiques, the repressive influence of the conservative Christian bodies, to say nothing of the conservative Muslim, Jewish, and other religious bodies? Is such an agenda even a flicker, a passing blip on the screen of their creditable ambitions? I wish I could anticipate affirmative answers, but the data seem to forbid it.

Conclusion

I have floated the case of sexual justice, women's rights to equality with men, as a provocation—a fillip to any Christians presuming to call themselves prophetic. With at least some awareness of the quixotic character of such a proposal, I have asked the churches to make their dialogues with the world religions include a frank criticism of the maltreatment of women that one finds in both the history and the doctrine of the leading interlocutors that Christians presently engage. My assumption has been that the rebound from this criticism, the requisite look at their own performances regarding women, would only help the Christian churches fulfill the ethical charges their God has laid on them in commissioning them to preach the gospel. Moreover, I have been cheered, rather than daunted, by the prospect of all major religious peoples looking hard at the plight of women and children, the poor and marginalized, and recognizing how much they have done to create or abet the great suffering of these groups.

I cannot picture the evangelical Christ moving in our present world gagged and blindfolded. I cannot imagine him not at least struggling to be a prophet to all the nations sickened by injustice, including prominently sexual injustice. I have to hear him calling all citizens of our now clearly single world order to repent of their sins against those considered less human than the male elites ruling most cultures. I have to note a blush of shame inflaming his cheeks as he contemplates what God's various peoples—all chosen, though clearly differently—have done against women, have failed to do for women. He is the vine vivifying many branches that have not wanted to live as genuine prophets do: denouncing social injustice and sponsoring a cult that makes creative, healing love the basic coin of the economy of salvation. He is the leader possessed of a vision of human dignity and equality that few of his followers, explicit or anonymous, have been willing to bear, let alone give their lives to promote. When that vision focuses on us, his ordinary layfolk, as well as on the patriarchs, cardinals, and upper-echelon superintendents of whom he may expect more, it registers a sorry reality. Perhaps the most relevant question is whether we shall have the stomach, the grit, to admit our unloveliness and at least try to change our depreciation of women.

I do not imagine such change making us shrill, hateful, impatient. I imagine it making us simply radical: people who desire to go to the depths of the divine love, whence Jesus drew forth his inmost identity and strength. What a lovely desire that would be! Suppose that we did follow the prophets of the various world religions and realize that all our happiness, as well as much nearly certain pain, resides in the light of God? Would we not clarify our human vocation considerably? That light is the candle that has shone in the darkness of depravity and never been overcome. That light comes with the voice that has never agreed to the abuse of women, children, the poor, the handicapped, any people different from the few holding political power and cultural prestige. That light is the source of the courage of the prophets, the spokespersons for God who have lived beyond fear.

If the light shines in our own darkness, and we realize that not even our stupidity or sin can overcome it, we too can become prophetic. We too can say that female infanticide, the physical abuse of the small and vulnerable, sexual mutilation, the failure to cherish the sexes equally, the repression of women's talents and freedom to determine their own destinies, and all the rest reek in the nostrils of God. We shall not fear to denounce the inability of women to stand alongside men as equals before Allah, or the talmudic Lord, or the Christ at the head of the Christian church. We shall not hesitate to exhibit the miseries of abortion, violence against homosexuals, writing off any race or ethnic group as uneducable, not fit for our mainstream. Without any sense of self-righteousness, we shall consider the actual behavior of the world religions the primary matter for interreligious examination and prophetic critique. Why? Because a glimpse of the light, a taste of the Spirit, will have made us want to speak the truth and be convicted by it. Is there a better life? Is there an alternative way to losing and finding oneself in God's love? I believe that all the genuine prophets say no, because I find that all the genuine prophets rejoice in the yes God has said to all her people, women as certainly and fully as men.

5

A Prophetic Challenge
to Men

JOHN TULLY CARMODY

The biblical prophets became passionately concerned about social justice and right worship. When the Word of God seized control of their minds and hearts, they had no choice but to demand attention to the plight of widows, orphans, strangers in the land—any people pained by unjust or careless treatment. As well, they had to insist that only the Lord deserves true worship, is so real (holy) that we have to love his mystery with our whole mind, heart, soul, and strength. Through more than 2,500 years, these prophetic instincts have prodded, chastened, and challenged all the children of Abraham. Again and again the Christian centuries have pulsed with movements of reform inspired by Amos and Hosea, Isaiah and Jeremiah. Without these movements, the often sorry Body of Christ no doubt would have seemed even sorrier. Without a vibrant prophecy for the year 2000, the followers of Jesus will serve their Lord shabbily, with little power, and to little good effect.

Where does one get a vibrant Christian prophecy? The question is not difficult to answer. If one reads the New Testament without blinking at the provocative behavior of Jesus in curing on the Sabbath, associating with tax collectors and whores, and condemning many members of the religious establishment as practically godless, an object lesson in prophetic behavior, prophetic existence, dances before one's eyes. It provides a dangerous, beguiling ballet, and one arguably at the heart of Christology: what it meant for Jesus of Nazareth to come, anointed in power, to proclaim the good news of God. Indeed, for God to seal this good news by resurrecting Jesus from the dead was for Jesus inevitably to become what J. B. Metz has called a "dangerous memory," what we might call a dangerous Lord living in the midst of the church and forcing it to be prophetic.

Second, we get a vibrant Christian prophecy from the Spirit of Christ,

the living Lord. The Spirit raised up the prophets of Israel. The Spirit led
Jesus into the wilderness and guided him to his consummation in Jerusalem.
The Spirit has been poured out over the church, establishing it in power.
Not only are all who are led by the Spirit children of God, all who are led
by the Spirit are shaped by prophetic power. To be led by the Spirit, or
have the Spirit make one's prayer with sighs too deep for words, and not
follow Jesus in reading the signs of one's times or challenging the corrupt
powers of one's day seems a contradiction in terms. Thus any vital contemplative prayer, participation in the liturgy, or endurance of evil in the Spirit
is likely to display a prophetic dimension. The God to whom the Spirit
brings us in prayer, like the resources that the Spirit makes available for
enduring evil, stands against both injustice and impure cult. To be brought
toward God is to be taken away from, to have one's face set against, the
ungodly powers of one's time — everything that cripples human existence
and conflicts with the good news that Christ was compelled to preach.

Third, we can get a vibrant Christian prophecy simply by making our
faith bear on what we read in the newspapers, what we see on television,
what we find on the streets of our crumbling cities, what we dismiss as
tainted in the deliberations of our church's authorities. The failure of doctrinaire capitalism, as of doctrinaire communism, reminds us that economics, whether in the United States, the former Soviet Union, or Somalia is
corrupt as long as it places ideas, or the profits of a few, over the crying
needs of the many. The seemingly endemic hatred we find in scenes from
what used to be Yugoslavia, what we continue to call Northern Ireland,
and what we might call tribal Africa reminds us that the main Christian
prophet required love of our enemies and forgiveness seven times seventy,
with no obvious exceptions.

The homeless people who disgrace the streets of most American cities
are the "poor of the Lord," first among those whom Jesus beatified. The
women and homosexuals treated shabbily in recent documents of churches
like my own Roman Catholic Church stand as prophetic indexes of how far
many holding Christian authority seem to live from the simple, radical love
of Jesus, who opened his arms to all God's people, especially those most
in pain. In a word, then, prophecy is as near as any suffering portion of
creation. Disciples with eyes to see, ears to hear, are bound to follow Jesus
in taking the side of the oppressed.

For the remainder of this short study, I want to concentrate on what a
vibrant Christian prophecy might require of Christian men and offer to
them. This concentration is not an effort to exclude women or domesticate
prophecy to the often narcissistic concerns of what some now call a "men's
movement." Rather, it is an effort to bring the tradition of biblical criticism — more specifically, biblical self-criticism — to bear on those who continue to hold great, probably inordinate power in the churches and most
of the world's cultures. If we look at the example of the evangelical Christ,
the energies characteristic of an intercourse with God guided by Christ's

Spirit, and the stark yet still strangely vivifying realities that mark current history as permeated by terrible suffering, what ought we to say to the men in the seven churches that Revelation uses to epitomize the Body of Christ? What can we intuit, and then work out, to beguile male followers of Christ into living by his dangerous memory and taking fitting risks of their own?

On the Movement of Men

Is Robert Bly the prophet come for the rescue of Christian men from much that makes them sad, sorry abusers of women and children, faithless cretins who hear little of their Master's news? I doubt it. I can muster as much delight in a Jungian fairy tale as most men, but I find the movement to make Bly's *Iron John* or Moore and Gilette's *King, Warrior, Magician, Lover* new scripture embarrassing. Certainly, men ought to probe the lesions in their psyches and embrace images that might heal them. Certainly, the many dysfunctions that have afflicted the modern family, indeed modern society as a whole, bear on the matter of what men have been able to be and do—for themselves, for women and children, for the cause of Christ. But the simple history of Gnosticism shows that little redemption comes from focusing on the human psyche and refusing to obey the instinct of John the Baptist that Christ must increase and the disciple decrease. Similarly, what I take to be simple common sense argues that men and women are coordinate, in such wise that to remove men from dealings with women, even for the sake of analytical study, is a faux pas.

Third, I am embarrassed when Christians, whom I think ought to know better, neglect the great themes of their holy forebears—prayer, penance, service of the poor, faith in truly divine life—for a psychological pottage. From the desert fathers through the Reformers and John of the Cross, the precious otherness of the living God makes traditional Christian spirituality a profound recreation of the human personality. Christ is the Word of God become human that we might gain redemption and divine life. Should we cash "divine life" out as a reentry upon the wildness that less refined, feminized men enjoyed as warriors and hunters? If I feel healed from painful memories of alienation from my father, have I entered upon the deathless existence of Father, Son, and Spirit?

Clearly, there is room for distinctions and qualifications in sophisticated answers to these questions, but equally clearly, I believe, men wanting a radical Christian faith and willing to educate themselves in its historical traditions are bound to conclude that much of what they find in current literature about "men's issues" is superficial, if not indeed simply drivel. The great issues continue to be how to overcome death and death-dealing evil. What Jesus said, did, suffered, and revealed about these issues, along the orchestral spectrum of their ontological, psychological, socioeconomic, and political levels, leaves Robert Bly behind, strumming a little banjo. Christian men are not going to find fulfillment by beating their chests in the wildwood. If the New Testament bears any valid witness, they are only going to find their lives by losing them in prophetic discipleship to the fiery Christ.

On the Self-Criticism of Men

When Christian men attend to the signs of their times and let such attention bend back in self-criticism, what are they likely to find? How does a prophetic demand that Christian men put aside privileges or powers that are proving to be engines of injustice assemble itself in the consciences of those willing to invite it to shape their faith? These are questions pointed enough to give us a beginning.

Many analysts of poverty, both around the globe and in the United States, underscore that women and children suffer the most. The "feminization of poverty" does not mean that no men are homeless, out of work, or hungry, but it does mean that men continue to fare better than women. How do men of Christian conscience abide this state of affairs? How ought the churches preach about it? My intuition is that men of Christian conscience do not abide the feminization of poverty well, that it rankles and troubles them. Apart from any macho sense that men ought to suffer hardship more generously than women (which the historical record seems to mock), I find a prophetic tenderness of affection. The concrete widow and orphan, freed from the status of stock figures calling to mind a generally unjust state of affairs, solicit the attention, the concern, the compassion of the generous follower of Jesus, in large part because Jesus went out of his way to heal the sick and uplift the downtrodden.

This solicitation opposes directly the hard-nosed, mean-spirited economic posture that has settled over corporate America. It asks for a wholesale "no!" to the proposition that the business of business is profits, or that the business of government is divesting itself of care for its citizens. Though they know they will surely be mocked, the men of prophetic temper whom I imagine following the evangelical Christ and challenging the churches to preach likewise can only smile and say that corporate America, professionally political America, is dumber than dirt about the gospel.

In the beginning, the gospel announces glad tidings for the poor and release for captives. The first beneficiaries of this proclamation ought to be the majority of those suffering from socioeconomic disorders: women and children. If male Christian church leaders want to demonstrate their courageous embrace of the dangerous memory of Jesus, they ought to make the amelioration of the plight of poor women and children their first order of social business. It is not wrong for them to do this with a touch of chivalry, or as an explicit venture in atonement for the sins of their patriarchal forebears, but the better instinct would be for them to do it as a simple reflex formed by contemplating the prophetic Christ. Christ emptied himself, thinking the form of God nothing to which to cling. Self-critical Christian men would seem handsome nowadays if they followed Christ and emptied themselves of the many forms, economic and political, that appear to exalt them over women and children.

A further step in self-critical programs that we might recommend to Christian men comes along when they note the analyses that feminist believers now present to them, sometimes suavely and sometimes not. (Naturally, the wrapping is less important than the gift it covers.) In the perception of women of faith that many men miss the wholeness of life at the center of the gospel stands a proposition well worth taking to heart. Men have to decide for themselves what is valid in this proposition and what not, as well as how they are to appropriate what is valid. Still, accepting the proposition as a challenge and invitation probably pleasing to the Spirit of Christ tends to open the self-criticism of men to depths, implications, degrees of acuteness that it might not reach on its own.

Consider, for example, the links between this feminist proposition and the dire state of the environment. One does not have to accept all the baggage of a radical ecofeminism to note the cogency of assimilating our recent domination of nature to patriarchal patterns through which men have tried to dominate women. Nowadays it is clear that we are dominating nature to the point where it is gasping for breath, parched for clean water, desperate to renew its primary ecosystems. The way of life developed in the industrialized nations and exported to the whole world as the ideal for which to labor seems incompatible with the endowment given us in nature. Nature will not support for another hundred years the uses to which we are presently forcing it. Nature is sickening, and if we persist in these uses, it will die.

The feminist critique that correlates these uses with stereotypically male drives for dominion is acute. Among the psychological resources of people trying to sort out the ecological crisis and reform the developed nations' worldviews, it may be nonpareil. I believe that Christian men, freed of the need to be served destructively by either nature or other people, freed by the example of Christ rather to serve nature and other people, do themselves and the environment a large favor when they take this feminist critique to heart. Whatever nuances they might have to enter, so that the critique fit either a given historical period or their own distinctive personalities, the main charge would remain highly revealing.

What, in fact, is the mentality that both ordinary citizens and entrepreneurial developers will have to acquire, if nature is to recover and posterity not appear imperiled? How, in practice, can the ministerial mentality of Christ create more generous, patient, helpful ways of dealing with the environment? Why, in their preaching of the gospel, are the churches saying little about either the radical simplification of life-style that the ecological crisis summons or the symmetry between this simplification and evangelical poverty? If they will ask themselves critical questions like these in a prophetic mode, Christian men can start to formulate positive responses to the challenges now offered them by feminist analysts.

Third and last, warfare remains with us in sufficient virulence to make questions of aggression, destructiveness, anger, violence, and the like all too relevant. Taking these questions to heart leads one into deep waters, for who can know with anything like full clarity the historical formation of the warrior, the hunter, the prototypical male battling on the frontiers where survival has been at stake? Who can say what aggression bodily factors such as hormones and social factors such as conditioning to kill for survival or defense have made inseparable from male humanity? Probably the better question for the Christian interested in the prophecy of Jesus is how to turn a proper aggression against the most daunting foes, evil and death. The prophecy of Jesus gained its sharp edge because he defeated death on his own terms. Opposing evil from the depths of his spirit rather than with destructive arms, Jesus became a credible, indeed the dazzling expression of the God in whom there is no darkness at all. Reflecting on this, Paul saw the main warfare to be with principalities and powers. Nowadays, we might say that the demons controlling the men who must have war live in their souls.

Certainly, jobs, money, past cruelties on the historical record, and many other "objective" factors go into the butcheries occurring recently in Eastern Europe, Africa, Asia, Latin America, and places closer to home. But men in love with the evangelical Christ do not lust for blood. No matter how hardened to political realities, such men will not sanction ethnic cleansing, rape, pillage, constant opposition to peacemaking because of pride or the will to power. So conversion remains completely relevant, wholly requisite. If converted to the prophetic vision of the evangelical Christ, men will not be led by their hormones or social conditioning into mindless violence, hopeless warfare. If serious about their Christian profession, they will not exempt themselves from the task of making peace, creating reconciliation, defining their manhood as enduring, even suffering painfully, rather than embracing an evil violence at odds with the Kingdom of God.

Summarily, then, the prophetic challenge that I would have the Christian churches offer to men is not to join a movement aping women's discovery of manifold oppression and concentrate on its psychological aspects. Rather, it is to refocus their energies on the courage of the evangelical Christ, who stood free of the various cooptings available in his time and served only the good news of his Father—the word of freedom his God compelled him to enact for the poor of his day. The selflessness of this task recommends it nicely to a narcissistic age. The power of the grace, the eternal love, available in the Spirit of the prophetic Christ remains the great hope of Christian believers. Do many men want to be Christian believers, more than baptized members of therapy groups? It's hard to say what the smile I imagine coming to the face of the Lukan Jesus as he hears this question means.

6

"Who Is There Big Enough to Love the Whole Planet?" (E. B. White)

WILLIAM SLOANE COFFIN

Of all Michelangelo's powerful figures, none is more poignant than the man in the *Last Judgement* being dragged down to hell by demons, one hand over one eye, and in the other a look of dire recognition. He understood, but too late.

It's a familiar story: Rarely do we see the truth that stares us in the face until it hits us in the face; a crisis is seldom a crisis until it is validated by disaster. Michelangelo was right: Hell is truth seen too late.

I recall his figure because I am convinced that we are all hell-bent unless we open our eyes and see the most significant event of the twentieth century, one as unheralded as was the birth of Christ two thousand years ago. I have in mind the birth of the world, and the fact that the world once born is going to continue to grow, claiming its own history, a right to its own economics, and politics and peace. The big news of the twentieth century is that henceforth it is the world as a whole that has to be managed, and not just its parts.

Until recently it was enough to be concerned with the parts, to worry that this part of the world couldn't protect itself against that part. Today it's the whole that can't protect itself against the parts.

In World War II, nations at war targeted one another. Today the whole world lives on the target of World War III. If we do not soon stop the modernization and proliferation of weapons of mass destruction, the whole planet will become a nuclear porcupine—or a dreary waste of ash and cinder, silenced by death. Likewise, if we do not soon evolve a lifestyle more considerate of the environment, we may all bake slowly in a stew of industrial pollutants. And if Abraham Lincoln was right, that a nation cannot long endure half-slave half-free, then it is unreasonable to expect the world long to endure, partly prosperous, mostly miserable.

In short, the planet is at risk, and in an order of magnitude never previously imagined. No longer is the survival unit a single nation or single anything; it is the entire human race plus the sky above and the earth beneath. Schoolchildren everywhere, beyond saluting their flags, should pledge allegiance "to the earth, and to the flora, fauna, and human life that it supports; one planet indivisible, with clean air, soil and water, economic justice, freedom and peace for all." And Christians everywhere must stop retreating from the giant social issues of the day into the pygmy world of private piety. The chief religious question is not "What must I do to be saved?" but rather "What must we all do to save God's creation?"

It is the religious community—Muslims and Jews as well as Christians— that has the saving vision. It is the ancient prophetic vision of human unity, now become an urgent pragmatic necessity. According to this vision, we all belong one to another, every one of us on this planet. That's the way God made us; from a Christian point of view, Christ died to keep us that way; our sin is always and only that we put asunder what God has joined together. Human unity is not something we are called to create, only to recognize and make manifest. Territorial discrimination has always been as evil as racial, as Pablo Casals recognized when he asked: "To love one's country is a splendid thing, but why should love stop at the border?"

Were religious believers truly to believe in the unity they profess, a unity universal and eternal, surely the world could move rapidly into a future far preferable to the predictable one.

But now we have to confront an irony profound and complicated. At the very moment in history when the mere notion of national sovereignty is about as obsolete as was "States' Rights" when Jefferson Davis preached it and millions fought for it, the two most powerful movements in the world are nationalism and racism.

Both can be attributed largely to sin: Once again we are putting asunder what God has joined together.

But it would be a mistake to leave it at that, not to recognize the many legitimate differences that exist within our common humanity. Nationalism, ethnicity, race, gender, our different sexual orientations—all have their rightful place, and the universalism, which is their opposite, tends to blur, deny, and too often repress what is particular about them. It is totally understandable that people want to preserve and deepen their roots in their own land, language and culture, and that they want to champion a gender or race that has for so long been so cruelly maligned. It should come as no surprise that everywhere people are asserting the particular over and against the universal. It is not even surprising that nations themselves are breaking up, for while the nation-state is clearly too small for the big problems of life, nation-states often appear too big for the small problems of life.

So the challenge to the churches is to seek a unity that celebrates diversity, to unite the particular with the universal, to recognize the need for roots while insisting that the point of roots is to put forth branches. What is intolerable is for differences to become idolatrous. When absolutized, nationalism and ethnicity, race and gender are reactionary impulses. They become pseudo-religions, brittle and small, without the power to make people great. Human beings are only fully human when they find the universal in the particular, when they recognize that all people have more in common than they have in conflict, and that it is precisely there, where what they have in conflict seems overriding, that what they have in common needs most to be affirmed.

Present national policies and national structures are not only incapable of solving worldwide problems, they in fact exacerbate them. The future is slipping from us like sand through our fingers. To preserve the planet we need minimally and immediately to moderate national sovereignty and increase global loyalty.

Americans have a helpful analogy in their history. After successfully declaring their independence from Great Britain, the original thirteen colonies decided to govern themselves according to the so-called Articles of Confederation. But the articles more mirrored than resolved the problems of the day. So our spiritual forebears quickly abandoned the Articles of Confederation in favor of a constitution which demanded the sacrifice of a certain amount of independence for the sake of a stronger, more effective whole.

The United Nations today is the Articles of Confederation. The United Nations Charter is a pre-atomic document. When the United Nations was organized, it was for an era that was already over. Said Albert Einstein: "The release of the power of the atom has changed everything except our way of thinking. Thus we drift toward a catastrophe of unparalleled magnitude."

Some time ago, a Latin American delegate at the UN observed wryly: "Around here (at the UN) things tend to disappear. If it's a conflict between two small powers and we deal with it, the conflict disappears. If it's a conflict between a small and a large nation, the small nation disappears. And if it's a conflict between two large nations, then the UN disappears."

The UN disappears because not one of the almost 180 states of the world has seen fit to surrender one iota of its sovereignty. The UN hasn't failed the world, it's the world that has failed the UN. The nations of the world have refused to see the truth staring them in the face. All have failed to make what we might call the magnum conceptual leap forward that the times demand.

To quote Einstein again: "Imagination is more important than knowledge." Bolder intellectual horizons would teach us not only to analyze the world as it is and ask "why"; they would also urge us to imagine the world as it might be and ask "why not?"

We need to imagine a world whose citizens will be as mindful of international law as they are of domestic law and so obey the decisions of the World Court at The Hague.

We need to imagine a world whose peacekeeping forces will be larger than any national force. Only so can there be genuine collective security where the strength of all is for the defense of each.

We need to imagine a world whose international agencies will be supported by an international income tax, based on Gross National Product or perhaps energy consumption. If this seems preposterous, let us recall that so did a national income tax when, at the turn of the century, it was being urged upon Americans by William Jennings Bryan.

We cannot imagine a world free of conflict, for the horizons of the world will always be darkened by dissension. But we can imagine a world free of violent conflict, free of toxic wastes, and one in which the yawning chasm that presently divides rich and poor would be greatly narrowed.

If all the above, and especially the vision of a world beyond war, seem hopelessly utopian, that may simply reflect how far we have slipped behind in a schedule we should have kept, had we been serious about saving the planet. Besides, isn't it better to work for a world that may seem too beautiful to be true than drift toward one too horrible to contemplate?

As the great issues of our time are all ethical, it would certainly help if churches and seminaries would cease trying to separate theology from ethics—which is always bad theology. How, after all, can you be holy without being moral? Isn't justice the moral test of spirituality? Important as is the purity of dogma, it is never as significant as the integrity of love. Creeds are signposts, love the hitching post. To deny the ultimacy of love is not a distortion of the Gospel, it's desertion. It is to use the God who made of one blood all nations of the earth to justify the continued spilling of that blood. What the churches, synagogues, and mosques need most to ponder is less of their many and differing creeds, more of a single ethic of global responsibility.

Such an ethic would address crucial tasks, which here I shall only outline. As earlier implied, the planet is threatened on three major fronts: (1) by the modernization and proliferation of weapons; (2) by the way we live in our environment as in a hotel, leaving the mess for others to clean up; and (3) by a Dickensian world of wretched excess and wretched despair. In positive terms, the conquest of war, the preservation of nature, and the pursuit of social justice must become, as Norman Cousins put it, "our grand preoccupation and magnificent obsession."

Above all, and at almost any risk, we must get the world beyond war. It is not enough to wish for peace. We have to *will* it: to pray, think, struggle for peace as if the whole world depended upon it, as indeed it does.

I am well aware that Jesus didn't tell the Roman centurion to leave the service, nor did John the Baptist tell the soldiers who came to be baptized to lay down their arms. But arms in John's day compared to arms in ours were as the lightning bug to the lightning.

First the testing and then the production of all weapons of mass destruction must cease. Let Christians remember that only God has the authority to end life on this planet; the only thing human beings have is the power. Disarmament must take place under stringent international inspection — on-site inspection without right of refusal.

Further, we have to call it unacceptable that any nation promote its foreign policy goals through the sale and transfer of weapons, and that arms of any kind be sold for commercial profit. Just as the first step toward the abolition of slavery was the abolition of the slave trade, so now the first step toward the eventual abolition of arms should be the abolition of the arms trade. The United Nations should immediately begin to monitor and publicize all sales and transfers of arms from one country to another.

As conventional weapons are conventional only in the sense of being nonnuclear, not nonlethal, wars should no longer be defined by the weapons used but by the harm done. And as the harm done by conventional weapons is morally so reprehensible, Christians should be prepared to resist all reasons advanced for waging war. It should be clear to them that to fight merely for national honor or interests is an act of religious infidelity. When religion is used to undergird militarism, then, like the man on the road from Jerusalem to Jericho, our faith has fallen among thieves who have stripped it of its meaning.

To save the environment — a second common task — we need an Earth Covenant, a form of Magna Carta for the earth. Such a charter would expand the Universal Declaration of Human Rights so that some of the ethical considerations that presently govern human relations will be extended to nature as well. In religious terms, we need to reconnect nature with nature's God with a focus more "cosmocentric" than anthropocentric. With Native Americans, we need to recognize our spiritual tie with every leaf and furry creature; with Orthodox Christians, to see ourselves not only as stewards but as "priests of Creation."

And thirdly, we need to go beyond charity. Charity is a matter of personal attributes; justice is a matter of public policy. Never can the first be a substitute for the second.

Here in America and in the Third World, the "haves" today have more than ever, while the "have nots" are more numerous and more undeniably miserable. If people have equal dignity, there cannot be such degrees of economic inequality. As William Penn said years ago: "It is a reproach to religion and government to suffer so much poverty and excess."

Communism in Eastern Europe failed in large part because it did not produce enough. But capitalism in the United States fails to share equitably the greater wealth it produces. Christians need to remember that privilege is often a matter of theft, that not only poverty but also superabundance can keep people in a subhuman state. And, of course, both communism and capitalism have proved devastating to the environment.

Earlier I suggested a new pledge of allegiance for school children. Let me offer another for young adults: "I pledge to seek only such employment as will benefit my fellow human beings and not harm the environment."

Let me close with a final thought. I have urged the need to chip away at national sovereignty and expand global loyalty. But I believe that global loyalty will be reached *through* patriotism, not by rejecting it. Christians simply cannot allow political leaders to hijack patriotism in the service of fervent jingoism. Basically there are three kinds of patriots. The bad patriots are the uncritical lovers and the loveless critics of their country. The good patriots are those who carry on a lover's quarrel with their country, a reflection of God's eternal lover's quarrel with the entire world.

Nationalism at the expense of another nation is as evil as racism at the expense of another race. Nevertheless, just as a man can love his wife without denigrating other women, so patriots ought to be able to love their country without disparaging others. I love America, and it is precisely because I love my country and want to promote its best interests that I want its citizens to recognize their interdependence with all nations, their need for common rather than national security, the worldwide need for disarmament, ecological legislation and greater economic justice.

Genuine love expands, it doesn't contract. True patriotism can only extend minds and hearts, extend them to the point where all citizens in every land will one day vote for a vision of human unity once so eloquently described by a candidate for the U.S. Presidency: "We travel together, passengers on a little space-ship, dependent on its vulnerable supplies of air and soil; all committed for our safety to its security and peace, preserved from annihilation only by the care, the work, and I will say, the love we give our fragile craft" (Adlai Stevenson).

To eyes that are open, this vision is a hope still visible, not yet beyond hand's reach. The world awaited can yet become a world attained.

Poems by Dorothee Soelle

A sort of love poem

A few more like you bob
not at all extreme
or drunk with expectations
but still armed
with the normal love for peace
they try to wean us from and order us to shed
bit by bit
to get us ready for their war
against the migratory birds

Of these you speak in a tone
not at all extreme
more like a new englander
but still with eyes
for the normal flyways of the birds
eyes they are trying to blind
if need be with gas

A few more like you bob
a few more like your friends
let's say a million more
and we could declare peace
on those who abolish it
turning brute force
against the migratory birds.

The Gift of Tears

Give me the gift of tears oh god
give me the gift of speech

Lead me out of the house of lies
wash me clean of my education
liberate me from my mother's daughter
take my barricades by storm
raze my intelligent fortress

Give me the gift of tears oh god
give me the gift of speech

Cleanse me of concealing the truth
give me the words to reach the person next to me
remind me of the tears the young student in göttingen wept
how can I speak if I've forgotten how to cry
make me wet
don't hide me any longer

Give me the gift of tears oh god
give me the gift of speech

Shatter my pride make me simple
let me be water that others can drink
how can I speak if my tears are only about me
take away my private property and the desire for it
give and I'll learn to give

Give me the gift of tears oh god
give me the gift of speech
give me the water of life

Alternative tv

The old man on the screen sang
in a loud and shaky voice
and had probably never been very clean
in addition he had hardly any teeth left
a miner with black lung
of course he spoke dialect and his grammar was bad
why after all should he
show his best side to the camera

When god turns on his tv
he sees old people like that
they sing
in a loud and shaky voice
and the camera of the holy ghost

shows the dignity of these people
and makes god say
that is very beautiful

Later
when we have abolished tv as it exists
and are allowed to look at the skin of aging women
and are unafraid of eyes
that have lost their lashes in weeping
when we respect work
and the workers have become visible
and sing
in a loud and shaky voice

Then we will see
real people
and be happy about it
like god

In Praise of Friendship

and what
       shall David do without Jonathan
       and Karl Marx without Engels
       and Mary without Elizabeth
       and Che Guevarra without Fidel

and what
       is to become of all of us
       without Bob and Sydney Brown

friendship is
       when Abraham bargains with God
       to save Sodom
       and haggles the Exalted down
       from fifty to ten righteous
       out of friendship

friendship is
       when the fisherfolk set their nets aside
       and go along without, you'd say, asking where
       The beginning of organization and struggle
       the end of a goalless life
       out of friendship

friendship is
    when Mary looks up Elizabeth
    and lingers till the time for abortion
    is past, and with it the morning retching
    something new is coming, something for everyone
    out of friendship

and what
    will David do without Jonathan
    and Karl Marx without Engels
    and Mary without Elizabeth
    and Che Guevarra without Fidel
    and Jesus without John

and what
    is to become of poor Dorothy
    amid eight million New Yorkers
    without Bob and Sydney Brown

                              *

Friendship is
    when you go into people's house
    and, playing the piano in your unexceptional way,
    you've gotten no one to listen much less talk about it.

Friendship is
    when you are absolutely sure
    they will never be nice to you.

Friendship is
    being available, no minding if you do
    able to talk without having to
    able to ask and
    not despairing when no answer's there.

Friendship is
    knowing you can go knocking late at night
    if ever they came looking for you —
    the Gestapo, the FBI, the Stasi

and what
    will David do without Jonathan
    and Karl Marx without Engels
    and Mary without Elizabeth
    and Che Guevarra without Fidel

and Jesus without John
and Dietrich without Eberhard

• • •

and what
    is to become of all of us
    without Bob and Sydney Brown

Music

Whenever I hear music on the radio
classical one-o-four-point-three
I am afraid of the breaks
my tongue goes dry
I stop talking dishwashing reading
I hear the quiet
hear the emptiness
in a time
that belongs neither to me
nor to Johann Sebastian nor Johannes
nor the sad little Franz from Vienna

A small time
when I forget to breathe because I am so afraid
that soon the Wall Street Report will attack me
and terrifying advice
what to buy
where to eat
how to invest my money
will batter me

I feel I have to
protect my friends
Johannes from Hamburg
and Ludwig from Bonn
and Philip Emmanuel
(my God, he was already melancholy enough)
I do believe you
that you love them
but I still want to protect them
from your tyranny
about walking eating investing money

and that small quiet time
I'm thinking the colleagues

from classical one-o-four-point-three
could use it
because forgive me we need time
to love one another
especially Wolfgang and Robert
and all who knew something
about the stillness after the last note
about the strange time
that belongs to no one
that is absolutely free
maybe you know the word
free

PART II

RESOURCES

7

Toward the Recovery of the Prophetic Power of the Reformed Heritage

RICHARD SHAULL

The life and thought of Robert McAfee Brown witness to the power of our Reformed heritage to motivate and orient social transformation. It thus seems quite appropriate, as we honor him here, that we reflect further on that prophetic heritage and how it can function to sustain our struggles for justice at this time.

My own awareness of this aspect of Reformed faith dates back to my early years in Brazil. Working with young people from various Protestant churches, I soon came to realize that, very frequently, those who responded most positively to what I was preaching and teaching about Christian social responsibility were from a Presbyterian background. When I returned to the USA a decade later and became involved with a new generation of social activities, I had a similar experience. And in conversation with them, they often told me that they grew up assuming that their Christian faith called for commitment to the struggle for justice, although this was not something they had been taught in their home or church. As this had been my own experience as well, I found myself struggling with the question: What is there in our heritage that awakens and sustains this concern for social transformation? To find an answer to it, I had to undertake a reexamination of much of our Reformed history and theology.

In my courses in American church history while a seminary student, I thought I had learned a great deal about the early Puritans, but what stood out in my memory in later years was their rigid Calvinist theology, their near obsession with church order and discipline, and their legalistic moralism. When I took a new look at them, I found that they frequently gave voice to the conviction that God had called them to build a new society in this new world. As John Winthrop put it, in "A Model of Christian Charity," "For we must consider that we shall be as a city upon a hill. The eyes of all people are upon us."

While this was not something my professors at Princeton or the church historians recommended by them had emphasized, I began to find that other historians not directly associated with the church were calling attention to it. I remember especially what Page Smith had to say about the vision and religious motivation of the early Puritans in the first volume of his *A People's History of the American Revolution*. Many of those who came to New England, he writes, had sacrificed wealth and position and were willing to face hardship and danger. But their primary motivation was not to escape oppression or even to be free to worship as they chose. "What drove them on so zealously, so fanatically, was a passion for the redemption of the world for and through their Lord, Jesus Christ."[1]

Consequently, these Puritans dedicated their energies to establishing not just a purified church but redeemed and purified communities. In a new historical situation, they felt compelled to modify old social forms and devise new ones. In their town meetings, they moved in the direction of what we now call "participatory democracy," as people gathered to discuss and seek solutions to common problems. Great emphasis was placed on providing educational opportunities for all. And whatever the limitations and failures of their efforts, what stands out is the boldness of their vision of a new world and the energy with which they worked at building it. And they had no doubt that their motivation and orientation were a direct outgrowth of their Calvinist faith.

When I came to the conclusion, as the result of my experience in Latin America, that systemic change was urgently needed, and was struggling with the question of how to deal with it theologically, I began to study the various European revolutions that have shaped our modern world. And I soon discovered something else that had somehow escaped those who taught me the history of the Reformed churches, that the Puritan descendants of John Calvin had played a major role in the English Revolution of 1648. But I learned this, not from Reformed historians but from a Jewish political scientist, Michael Walzer. In *The Revolution of the Saints*[2] he showed that, behind this revolution, were pastors and lay persons whose experience of salvation in Christ had led them to undertake what Stephen Marshall called "great works," "the planting of a new heaven and a new earth among us." A profound spiritual transformation had produced men who, according to Walzer, were dedicated to "destroying the established order and reconstructing society according to the Word of God."[3]

What most fascinated me in all this was the intimate connection between spiritual renewal and radical politics. Here were people with a vital and profound faith in Jesus Christ. Their preaching centered on the power of the Gospel to create a new human being, as those who placed complete trust in a merciful and sovereign God were empowered to organize and discipline their lives around a new center and commitment. And it was this intense spiritual life that produced "a fierce antagonism to the traditional world and the prevailing pattern of human relation"[4] and led those so oriented to dedicate their energies to the struggle to transform both church and society.

It is thus hardly surprising that Puritan preaching had a strong appeal to many who felt alienated from the established order, or that this faith and community had the power to reorganize the lives of alienated people around a new set of values and a new vision of society. Conversion led to a radical critique of and break with a social and political order seen as contrary to God's will, and also to dynamic involvement in the struggle to create a new order. And participation in such a community of faith sustained those who were persecuted, as they were forced to give up their professional careers, lose their economic security, and, in many instances, go into exile. Thomas Hobbes well understood the danger they represented for the established order when he declared: "Had it not been much better that these seditious ministers, which were not perhaps one thousand, had been all killed before they had preached?"[5]

Turning from the Puritans to Calvin, I made another interesting discovery. From my first reading of the *Institutes*, I had been captivated by his interpretation of the biblical story as a great drama of redemption in three acts: God's gracious action in the creation of the world and of human beings; the fall and its consequences; and God's redemptive work of restoration in and through Jesus Christ. But what I had seen clearly before was that this restoration has to do with all aspects of life and calls for the complete transformation of historical existence. In the words of André Bieler, in his thorough study of *La Pensée Economique et Sociale de Calvin*,

> The Reformation of Calvin was a total reformation of the life of human beings in this world, considered both from the point of view of their individual existence and their collective life. For Calvin, in effect, there is no doubt that the Word of God is addressed to the whole man, in his present as in his future life, in his soul as in his body, in his spiritual life as in his material life, in his personal being as in his life in society. When God speaks, he meets man in the totality of his being and becoming. His voice is addressed to him as well as to humanity, to the universe and the entire creation; all that is profane becomes sacred; nothing escapes from the design, from the judgment, or from the love of God.[6]

To be called to participate in this redemptive process meant, for Calvin, to strive constantly not only to obey God but also to work to bring all of life into such obedience. And in a fallen world, that implied the radical transformation of the church as well as of society, "so that the kingdom of Jesus Christ may flourish by the power of His Word."[7]

In the academic world in which I have moved for most of my life, the articulation of such a radical perspective does not usually lead theologians to risk their careers and even their lives in social struggles. In Calvin's case it did. This conservative humanistic scholar, who yearned for the quiet life of scholarship, had every opportunity to pursue a brilliant career. But from the moment of his conversion, he chose to identify himself with a small band of vagabond, persecuted and marginal people. He took a stand in defense of those unjustly oppressed, without counting the cost. As a result, he was soon forced to give up the position he held, face persecution as a subversive and live in exile. More than this, he took on the thankless task of attempting to reconstruct the life of the city of Geneva according to the Word of God, in face of bitter opposition.

What could possibly lead a brilliant theologian to follow this path? I think there is only one answer: his compelling experience of the presence and power of a gracious God in his own life and in the world. Calvin appropriated Martin Luther's great discovery of justification by faith, grounded in the unlimited mercy of God, available directly to all who believe. This, for Calvin, meant also an amazing sense of the closeness of a God in whom one could have absolute trust. "What is more consonant with faith than to recognize that we are naked of all virtue, in order to be clothed by God? That we are empty of all good, to be filled by him? That we are slaves of sin, to be freed by him? Blind, to be illumined by him? Lame, to be made straight by him? Weak, to be sustained by him?"[8]

But for Calvin, as we have seen, this merciful God was acting in history to redeem and restore a fallen creation. Thus, to live by God's mercy and grace meant to have complete trust in God's redemptive action, not only in one's own life but also in the world, and thus to be free to give oneself totally to the obedience of love. Those caught up in this experience and mission were thus freed from the anxiety that comes with undue preoccupation with one's own spiritual state; justification by faith became the basis for a dynamic movement toward the world. The liberation experienced by the individual believer was a foretaste of the liberation of the world.

In a time of rapid social change, when an old order was in deep crisis and a new one had not yet been born, those who lived by this faith in a sovereign God were not unduly concerned about the collapse of trusted social structures and the crisis of traditional values. Captivated by a vision of a world being restored through Christ, they could sit loose to the past and look toward the future with hope. Their faith exposed as idolatrous all attempts to absolutize past achievements or to use the name of God to shore up structures of injustice. And, as Calvin and those associated with him in Geneva demonstrated, those who lived by this faith knew that they were called to respond to the love of God by struggling for justice, which involved not only the radical transformation of established institutions and structures but also the creation of new ones.

If these prophetic elements are at the heart of our Reformed faith and an essential part of our history, we should find ourselves drawing on them more and more as we become increasingly aware of what Calvin called "established disorder" and the tremendous suffering caused by social injustice. And as we appropriate more of the resources offered by this heritage for motivating and orienting our struggles for social transformation, we should find that our spiritual life is enriched, our commitment to the justice struggle is deepened, and our faith communities are revitalized.

And yet, this is not what we now see in our Reformed churches. Over the last fifty years, theologians in Europe and North America have done an extraordinary job of recovering the rich theological heritage of the Reformation and re-articulating it in contemporary terms. In our Presbyterian churches, it has been given a central place in Sunday school curricula and other educational efforts. But the impact of all this on congregational life has been minimal.

Churches in the Reformed tradition seem to be as much at home within the value system and the structures of the established order as other mainline denominations. And in recent years, the same Calvinist theology that once motivated and oriented those struggling for a radical transformation of society has frequently been used as a weapon against those with such commitments, and has even been drawn on for something Calvin vigorously condemned, the idolatrous sacralization of values and institutions of the established disorder.

Does this mean that a prophetic heritage, such as that of Calvin and the early Puritans, however great its past achievements, can have little value or power in our struggle today? I don't think this conclusion is warranted. But I am convinced that such a heritage can come alive and become a resource for us only when we stand where those prophets stood, only as we experience the crisis of our time and feel as intensely as they did the corruption and injustice of the existing order—only as we are willing to suffer with those who suffer and respond to the God who addresses us in the midst of it. Then, and only then, will we be in a position to hear the witness of the prophets who have gone before us and learn from them.

This is, in fact, already happening in some Reformed churches. In Taiwan, South Korea, and South Africa, for example, a number of church leaders as well as groups of lay persons and pastors have taken strong stands against racism and other forms of social injustice, as well as against governmental repression, and on occasions have paid a high price for it. And, as they have taken these steps, their own spiritual life has been enriched and their churches have been renewed. They have also discovered that their Reformed theology addresses the crucial social issues they are facing and that it is indeed, in their situation, a theology of liberation. What this has meant in South Africa is clearly spelled out by Professor John W. de Gruchy in his Warfield Lectures at Princeton in 1990, *Liberating Reformed Theology*.[9]

In the USA, we have witnessed the emergence, in many of our churches, of small groups made up primarily of lay women and men who have felt compelled to work together to change U.S. policy toward Central America and other third-world countries, to aid the homeless and other victims of poverty here at home, or to take part in other struggles for peace and justice. They have taken this step motivated by their Reformed faith and are eager to find ways to draw further on their religious heritage through biblical and theological studies. No one that I know has made a greater contribution in this area than Robert McAfee Brown, through his writing, speaking and personal involvement in these struggles.

If we want to encourage and contribute to these auspicious developments, we must, I believe, learn another lesson from Calvin. He understood that the radical witness called for by our faith can only happen if the church itself is *re-formed*, and he set about doing that with passion. Perhaps the time has come for us to realize that a new reformation is called for, and that this can happen only if we dedicate much of our energy today, as Calvin did in his time, to the formation of alternative communities of faith among those who are responding to the moving of the Spirit on the frontiers of the struggle for change.

As we undertake this task, we will realize that something else, even more demanding, is required of us. A prophetic heritage can enlighten and empower us today only as it is *recreated*. In Brazil, thirty years ago, I was shocked when young people in our churches, who had become involved in social struggles, confessed to me that the theology of the sixteenth century that I was teaching them, even when re-articulated by neo-orthodox scholars, did not speak compellingly to them. More recently, I have heard the same thing from many of those who are dynamically involved in movements for peace and justice. They are motivated to such action by their faith, but the theological categories and system of thought in our Confessions no longer name their world or serve to guide their actions.

This is not something any of us want to hear. Our theological training has prepared us to master and pass on a tradition, not to recreate it. And we can hope to engage in such creative work only as we move to the frontiers of struggle where the old order is passing away and allow ourselves to be captivated by a new vision; only as, from this perspective, we dare to question our most cherished assumptions, experience incoherence, and learn by trial and error. Moreover, the task of theological recreation is further complicated by the fact that, for Calvin, the supreme reality was an overwhelming experience of the closeness, majesty and redemptive presence and action of God in daily life. Is there anything that seems farther from our experience today than this?

I struggled with this question for many years after returning to the USA, for what I found so often in our mainline churches was either the absence of any vital or compelling experience of God or the idolatrous worship of a god who was expected to guarantee the self-centered life of privileged individuals. But all this changed dramatically when I returned to Latin America and came into close contact with the Christian Base Communities.

There, among the poorest and most marginal people, many of whom were facing persecution or risking their lives daily in the struggle for liberation, I was amazed to find many who had a sense of the closeness of

God and spoke quite naturally about God. Among those whom we might expect to be dehumanized by poverty and suffering, I found certain richly human qualities which they quite simply referred to as gifts of God: their spirit of quiet confidence and hope, of communion and sharing, of joyfulness and celebration.[10] Among Pentecostals and other neo-evangelicals living in extreme poverty and marginalization, I frequently found a similar experience of complete confidence and trust in a divine Presence and Power moving in their midst, healing, sustaining and empowering them. And I soon realized that often those of us who shared their lives and struggles found ourselves spiritually renewed, as well.

Moreover, among a number of those who, like myself, had come into closer proximity with the poor and their suffering, I realized that something else was happening. As we became more aware of the fact that they were deprived of almost everything we considered absolutely essential for a full human life, and as we got closer to their pain and suffering, our consciences were awakened and profoundly disturbed. We sensed that a claim was being laid upon us. In and through our encounter with the poor, we were being addressed. We were being called upon to respond, and this call had a transcendent dimension to it. God was addressing us, and as we responded, we found ourselves on the threshold of a new experience of the presence and power of God in our lives, as well.[11]

What can we conclude from all this? Is it possible that our experience of the absence of God has been due to the fact that all along we have been looking for God in the wrong place? That God has been and now is present in the world, but primarily among those whom we consider outcasts, the victims of exploitation and injustice? And could it be that, as we move toward them and respond to the claim of conscience, we might also find ourselves embarking on a new venture of faith?

If we dare to respond to this challenge, we may discover that our Reformed heritage will take on new importance for us as we strive to recreate it. We may not find much of Calvin's language about God very helpful for us, but as we have a new experience of the God who meets us in the struggle of the poor for life, we may find it well worth our while to explore the breadth and depth of Calvin's witness to the closeness of a God present and active in our personal lives and in history, for the radical transformation of the world.

Notes

1. *A New Age Now Begins* (New York: McGraw Hill, 1976), p. 21.

2. Michael Walzer, *The Revolution of the Saints* (Cambridge, Mass.: Harvard University Press, 1965).

3. Ibid., p. 1.

4. Ibid., p. 302.

5. Quoted in ibid., p. 114.

6. André Bieler, *La Pensée Economique et Sociale de Calvin* (Genève: Librairie de L'Universitè, 1959), p. 179.

7. Preface to Olivetan's New Testament, in Calvin, *Commentaries*, Joseph Haroutunian and Louise Pettibone Smith, eds. (London: SCM Press, 1958), p. 72.

8. "Prefatory Address to King Francis I of France, in *Institutes of the Christian Religion*, ed. John T. McNeill, tr. Ford Lewis Battles (Philadelphia: Westminster Press, 1960), p. 13.

9. John W. de Gruchy, *Liberating Reformed Theology* (Grand Rapids: Eerdmans Publishing Co., 1991).

10. For a fuller development of this, on the basis of the experience and reflection of Christians in the midst of suffering in Latin America, see my chapter, "The Redemptive Suffering of the Poor," in Francis A. Eigo, ed., *Suffering and Healing in Our Day* (Villanova: Villanova University Press, 1990).

11. This is a central theme in Frederick Herzog's *God-Walk: Liberation Shaping Dogmatics* (Maryknoll, N.Y.: Orbis Books, 1988).

8

Catholic Wellsprings for the Prophetic Imagination

JOHN COLEMAN

"Those who say that religion has nothing to do with politics do not know what religion means," Gandhi notes in his autobiography.[1] To no one's surprise, Catholicism, as the oldest religious, cultural and organizational variant of Western Christianity, has had much (perhaps too much!) to do with politics. All too often, alas, cynically and realistically, Catholicism's overture to politics has reflected the tone caught in the remarks of Peter Nichols, the long-time *Times* of London Vatican observer: "Politics enters the Vatican's thinking only indirectly. The object is to win and preserve the best position for the church. ... What it all comes down to is that the Vatican is against what is against its interests, and most of all it is against a persecuting power."[2] The Vatican's unseemly haste in concluding a *concordat* with Hitler and its exchange of diplomatic relations with Japan during the Second World War feed the kind of cynicism Nichols reflects.

This same note of *realpolitik* is struck by Gunther Lewy. "In any crucial situation, the behavior of the Catholic Church may be more reliably predicted by reference to its interests as a political organization than by reference to its timeless dogmas."[3] I begin my reflections on Catholic wellsprings for a prophetic imagination on this somber note as a reminder that the institutional interests of Catholicism have, and will continue to, put a brake on its prophetic imagination. Do not misinterpret me. My intent, in this assertion, is not primarily cynical.

Indeed, I am willing to defend the importance and usefulness of Catholicism's maintaining a ramified bureaucracy and organizational structure, as well as defending its institutional interests as a transnational actor in world politics. By keeping itself intact and viable as a transnational institution, the Catholic Church—as became obvious in Poland and the Philippines in the early 1980s—has remarkable diplomatic and organizational

resources to tilt the balance in world politics toward an increasing respect
for human rights, the rule of law, disarmament and the maintenance of a
fragile world order of peace. It can and has, somewhat consistently, used
its vast network of caritative associations to bring humanitarian relief to
refugees. It employs its presence in international forums, such as the United
Nations or the International Labor Organization, to plead for a tolerably
more just world order of trade, aid, and development.

But this important work is the task more of clerical statesmen and dip-
lomats than of prophets. The former aim at making our world a little less
unjust, a little more cooperative. They look to what Reinhold Niebuhr used
to call "the achievement of a rough justice here below" rather than to what
the scriptures call prophecy. To achieve this undeniable and desirable
human good of rough justice, however, church leaders on occasion come
in conflict with their prophets. Nor do church leaders scruple, on far too
many occasions, to quiet, at times totally to still, the more prophetic voices
at the grass roots or shunt them aside.[4] Perhaps in no other place is a
prophet without honor (until after his or her death, when they may be
canonized as saints!) than in highly placed Roman Catholic ecclesiastical
circles.

Catholic Social Teaching

The transnational institution, with its legitimate and undeniable organizational interests, is also a transnational culture. It does not restrict itself
to prudent, even if mainly humane, diplomacy and humanitarian work. The
church also enunciates a broader mandate for the good society in Catholic
social teaching. Anchoring its social vision in the inviolable respect for
human dignity and a moral sense of deep human solidarity beyond national
borders, Catholic Social Teaching injects an ethical dimension into politics,
trying to raise the political order beyond its present levels to higher visions
of the common good and world order and justice.

In Catholic Social Teaching the political order stands under the judgment of the common good. The economic order is assessed by what the
economy does for, with, and to people. The cultural order is called to prize
pluralism and the rights of a people to its own language, literature, cultural
mores and social representation. The international order is seen as needing
to build up international cooperative authorities which envisage an international common good.

Catholic Social Teaching adds to a *realpolitik* seeking a rough justice a
more visionary and humane spirit of cooperative justice.[5] Yet praiseworthy
and sane as is the Catholic social vision for a just, cooperative and participatory society, Catholic Social Teaching also stops somewhat short of what
the scriptures call prophecy. Rarely does it engage in utopias, imaginative
visions of alternative ways of living in society. It nuances or softens its
denunciations of injustice to gain a hearing in the wider society and to have

there some impact, to leave some leaven. It tailors its religious vision to humbler standards accessible to the well-meaning men and women of good will. "Thus speaketh the voice of reason and humane common experience" is the more likely appeal of the rhetoric in Catholic Social Teaching than the more dauntingly prophetic, "Thus speaketh the Lord."

In any event, even those, such as myself, who deeply treasure the legacy of Catholic Social Teaching rarely imagine that it feeds a deep prophetic imagination as such. Few of our most redoubtable latter-day prophets — Dorothy Day, Thomas Merton, Jean Vanier, Oscar Romero, Helder Camara, Daniel Berrigan, Gustavo Gutiérrez — claim that Catholic Social Teaching represents the primary well from which they slake their prophetic thirst. It was not from this source that their prophetic imaginations and saintly service sprang.

What, then, constitute the main Catholic wellsprings for the prophetic imagination? Before I enumerate them — and I claim they are three — I want to make an important disclaimer, one I learned from Robert McAfee Brown, whom we rightly honor as a prophet in these essays (although he would disclaim the title). On one occasion, Bob Brown and I served on an ecumenical panel to discuss Catholic vs. Protestant visions of justice. Brown refused to be pigeonholed into a too narrowly partisan and/or parochial "Protestant" camp. He averred that he wanted to honor truth, vision and the striving for justice wherever they were found in Christianity. As a balanced and ecumenical Christian, he would honor "The Protestant Principle" and the "Catholic substance." With the Reformers, he would proclaim the permanent relevance of the Reformers' slogans: "Let God be God"; "The church is always in need of conversion and reform"; "All, at root, is gift and grace." Brown would join the Reformers' concern with the *proclamation* of God's justice with the Catholic emphasis on the *manifestation* in history and everyday symbols and sacramental events of God's presence, mercy, and gentle enabling power.[6]

Following Brown, an ecumenical Catholic will learn as much from Protestant prophets (e.g., Dietrich Bonhoeffer and the Calvinist heroes and heroines who protected Jews, in the most taken-for-granted way, in their villages in France) as from the Catholic Franz Jagerstatter in Austria, who refused to serve in Hitler's wars (against, let it be said, the "prudent" counteradmonitions of his bishop), or the heroic Jesuit martyrs of El Salvador. I am going to claim that three underground streams feed the Catholic (or should I simply say "Christian"?) wellsprings of the prophetic imagination. These three are: (1) a human contrast experience of injustice; (2) the scriptures and the personal encounter with the Risen Jesus; and (3) the Catholic way of combining the prophetic and the mystical.

A Human Contrast Experience of Injustice

Edward Schillebeeckx has written eloquently about the *humanum*. He claims that *"extra mundum nulla salus"* — outside this world, there is no salvation. Being saved means being saved in history by the God who acts in history; it entails being freed from the injustices of *this* world of sin and its despising of God's image. Schillebeeckx is wary about any too circumscribed and foreclosed (and foreclosing) definition of the human, and is thus wary of any too-closed "natural-law" vision of the essence of the human. What it means to be human changes its contours in time and context as much as it contains transhistorical content.

For this great Flemish theologian and humanist, we can sometimes be much more sure what the human will no longer allow (even if it is built deeply into cultural institutions and mores) than what the positive content of the human as such may be. The human is the image of God, the imageless one, the transcendent one. The human, too, has a transcendent and growing character. What it means to be human is still, in many respects, to be discovered.

By a contrast experience, Schillebeeckx points to a vivid sense of what can no longer be allowed to go on, that to which I must cry a strong no as a violation of the image of God, of the *humanum*.[7] Obscurely and perhaps only intuitively, Christians came to see that slavery (no matter how benignly practiced or widely accepted) was unworthy of the *humanum*. John Woolman and Sojourner Truth set themselves against the societally accepted human practice because of a vivid contrast experience of what the human should be. They shouted, insisted: This can no longer go on (no matter how unrealistic at this moment it may seem to root out the deeply entrenched societal institution of slavery). This practice violates and does sacrilege to God's own image and likeness. Catholics were not in the forefront (to put it gently) of the anti-slavery movement. They (even the Popes who eventually condemned the practice in the nineteenth century) had to learn from the earlier prophetic witness of Protestants, especially the Quakers.

In our own time, men and women see that paternalism and patriarchalism, which deny the effective equality of women in imaging God and Christ, can no longer be countenanced. They push at and fight the societal institutions that enshrine and embody the denial of women's dignity (including — as did a gentle and lovely prophetess nun, Theresa Kane, speaking to the Pope in Washington, D.C. — that denial within the church itself). Others are coming to see, with Pope Paul VI and John Paul II, that war as we practice it can no longer be accepted (no matter what the arguments for its limited use in *realpolitik*), and they turn to a consistent pacifism. They embody, as prophets, the not-yet and say it can become even now part of the already realized redemption in Christ.

For some today, the obscenity of legal maneuvers which brought Robert Harris in and out of a California gas chamber lead them to say: This can go on no longer. No more capital punishment. I is unworthy of the humans whom we kill and the humans who must do the killing. Nor can we simply wait until "reasonable men and women see it is so." In the present climate of political opinion in the United States, that would take a very long time, indeed. The prophet disrupts *realpolitik*, anticipates what current institutions cannot totally engage, in the name of his or her contrast experience of the shameful defacement of the *humanum* — the only acceptable image the Hebrew scriptures allow for Yahweh. Sometimes, as in ecological issues, the prophet tries to anticipate what humans are called to, destined for — a cohabitation of this planet with the variety of species and environments which give glory and pleasure to their creator God. In the Catholic world, today — especially in Latin America — latter-day prophets decry the treatment of the poor as nonpersons. They are willing to disrupt and grind to a halt the ordinary economic laws of the functioning economy (by resisting the "legal" land takeovers by agribusiness in Brazil) or the functioning political system.

Sometimes the contrast experience comes from a deep reading and immersion in the scriptural vision, as when someone probes the depth meaning of Matthew 25 or the Parable of the Good Samaritan. But, as the examples of slavery or the movement to honor the full equality of women show, the contrast experience can go against practices that were not directly condemned by scripture. The contrast experience which says, "This is unworthy of the *humanum*," is open, then, to nonbelievers who can be prophets in our midst. But for the Christian prophet, the deepening of the meaning and interpretation of the contrast experience finds its most profound continuing nurture in the scriptures.

Scriptural Prophecy

It continues to surprise me that long ages of Christianity seemingly missed the obvious preferential option for the poor, the marginalized and the outcast in the Hebrew scriptures and the New Testament. The contrast experience can lead to a new reading of the scriptures. Indeed, every great prophet or prophetic movement (since prophecy can be found in movements as well as individuals, and it is easier to be a prophet if one has the support of community, others spurring us on to courage and boldness) rereads the scriptures in terms of the prophets of the Hebrew scriptures and Jesus as the eschatological prophet of the end days.

Whether it was Saint Martin, discovering that in giving his cloak to the poor he was giving it (in an echo of Matthew 25) to Christ; or Saint Francis embracing poverty and humiliations to be close to the crucified Christ, whose stigmata he bore; or Dorothy Day in her writings, meditating on passages of scripture about hospitality to the poor, scripture has nurtured the great Catholic prophets. Daniel Berrigan echoes Jeremiah and the Book of Revelation. Dom Helder Camara speaks eloquently of Jesus' compassion for the multitude. Mother Teresa finds inspiration in the healing stories of the gospels.

Finding in scripture the radical source of prophecy does not discriminate between Catholics and Protestants. To be sure, popular stereotypes (based on real evidence of divergent practices) place Protestantism closer to scripture than Catholicism.[8] But this generally apt stereotype can degenerate into a caricature. To be sure, Catholics place scripture within the wider ambit of the church which proclaims and lives the scriptures. But in Catholic liturgies and lectionary readings for the liturgy, in most of Catholic preaching and, especially, in Catholic spirituality, scripture is central. Whether it be the Spiritual Exercises of Saint Ignatius (really, a methodical meditation on the gospels) or the great art tradition of the medieval churches (the scriptures, if you like, in pictures), scripture has always nurtured and brought forth Catholic prophecy wherever it exists.

I was once engaged in a case study of an upper-middle-class (mainly Republican) Presbyterian church in Massilon, Ohio, which chose to become a sanctuary church (i.e., to break the law in order to offer hospitality to "illegal" aliens who claimed to be "political" refugees while the United States government chose to see them as "economic" refugees). We were interested in the anomaly that this church of upstanding patriots had chosen to break the law. What led them to this improbable prophetic choice? It became clear to us that the main factor was a consistent preaching on and appeal to the Good Samaritan motif in scripture. What the politics of the congregation would never have allowed, its reading of scripture made possible.[9]

It is my conviction that the prophetic books of the Hebrew scriptures represent a kind of canon within the canon, a key to understanding the scriptures. It is no less my conviction that Jesus can best be understood as in the line of the prophets. Like other Christians, Catholic prophets are both spawned and nurtured by familiarity with and deepening in the scriptures. If the contrast experience, perhaps, comes from a source outside the scriptures, the way a Christian prophet will enact that contrast experience (e.g., nonviolently, with love for the enemy whose injustice is opposed, with humility, and so forth) will be shaped by a spirituality rooted in living the scriptures. At least one great modern Catholic prophet, Oscar Romero, would seem to have come to his contrast experience mainly through the scriptures. They opened his eyes to the degradation of human dignity in El Salvador that could not be allowed to continue. For others, the initial contrast experience, unmediated directly by scripture, will open their eyes to parts of the scripture which, heretofore, they misread or misunderstood.

The Mystical-Prophetic in Catholic Prophecy

As the American theologian David Tracy has powerfully argued, the scriptures contain at least two different readings of the common narrative of the New Testament. He names these two readings "the prophetic" and "the mystical." Tracy locates the differences, in the gospel genre, in the Synoptics, on the one hand, and John, on the other. In the Pauline epistles you find a conflation and synthesis of the two readings. In the gospel of

Mark, there is a strongly prophetic sense of history as rupture, break, discontinuity, even apocalyptic. In John, however, one encounters a more meditative and mystical rereading of the common passion narrative. In John, one discovers a new construal of God-as-love manifesting the inner life of God in the sign Jesus Christ and disclosing to the self the power and command to love as God loves.

As a somewhat justified stereotype, Catholicism has tended to maintain a closer kinship to the mystical tradition than Protestantism has. Not, of course, that that tradition is totally absent in Protestantism. Importantly, the mystical tradition of spirituality (alive and well in Catholicism) can militate against the prophetic imagination, tame it, cause it to lay greater stress on union now rather than on the necessary ruptures of history. The Christian mystics only rarely cultivated the prophetic imagination.

Tracy pushes the differences in an enlightening way:

Can a mystic properly read a prophetic text becomes a necessary question for the Christian as soon as one acknowledges John's rereading of the synoptic passion narrative. The same question recurs when the Wisdom tradition and the prophetic traditions give their different readings of the common narratives of the Hebrew Scriptures.

The strong sense of agency (and thereby freedom) of the prophetic reading of the common narrative can sometimes be challenged by the new Johannine model of a loving, meditative self-losing-and-gaining-itself-in a-new-union-with-the-God-now-construed-as-love in John. Yet such a challenge is not discontinuity. As both the neo-Platonist theologies and the classical love-mystics sensed, in John a new sense of freedom-as-love discloses a new possibility for understanding the self as agent. Neither the Christian prophet nor the mystic can live easily with one another. Yet, as the liberation, political, and feminist theologians now insist, only a mystico-prophetic construal of Christian freedom can suffice. Without the prophetic core, the struggle for justice and freedom in the historical-political world can too soon be lost in mere privacy. Without the mystical insistence on love, the spiritual power of the righteous struggle for justice is always in danger of lapsing into mere self-righteousness and spiritual exhaustion.[10]

If I read Tracy correctly, he is reminding us of a tension, strongly felt in Catholicism, between the mystical and the prophetic. If the tension is not resolved, the mystical can tame the Catholic prophetic imagination, divert it into other channels. As he cryptically puts it, "Neither the Christian prophet nor the mystic can live easily with one another." Throughout most of Catholic history, this tension has not been resolved. The two impulses, mystical and prophetical, have lived side by side.

If there is anything remarkably new in our own time in terms of the Catholic prophetic imagination, it would be the way in which liberation theologians (Gustavo Gutiérrez at the forefront, but also Jon Sobrino) have pioneered, as prophets, in writing literature about spirituality which insists, against the danger of privatization in the Catholic mystical tradition, that the usual designation for any retrieval of the mystical traditions in Catholicism must be denominated "the mystical-political." I do not see the same emphasis in liberation theologians from the Protestant tradition. Hence, of the three wellsprings for the Catholic prophetic imagination, this is the one that is, perhaps, the most "typically" Catholic.[11] The Catholic penchant for both-and rather than either-or thinking (what David Tracy calls the analogical as opposed to the dialectical imagination) forces Catholics to forge a unity between the mystical and prophetic imaginations. Precisely this attempt at synthesis, I would argue, might be the main Catholic contribution to the prophetic imagination.

In the end, every prophet, like Robert McAfee Brown himself, will be gripped by God, constrained to face squarely the evil of the day seen as a contrast experience to the *humanum* and empowered by hope to proclaim, already, here and now, the Kingdom of God which Jesus preached. The prophet, too, will know, as Gutiérrez so well puts it in his now-classic treatise on spirituality, *We Drink from Our Own Wells*, that our actions for justice, our sense of the now-demanded new face for the *humanum*, will depend on a mystical union of God with us. For, "Unless God build the prophetic house we would construct, we labor in vain." Ultimately, as Jesus reminded us, unless we be grafted onto his vine and fed by his sap, "without him we can do nothing."

In praising Robert McAfee Brown in these essays, we are engaging in a very Calvinist project (one which, as a Jesuit and long time friend of Bob's, I gladly take part in, since, fortunately, Ignatius' motto is almost verbatim the same as Calvin's): *ad soli Dei gloriam.*[12] For the prophetical-mystical reminds us that it is God who perfects the work.

Notes

1. Mahatma Gandhi, *An Autobiography or The Story of My Experiments with Truth*, M. Desai, tr. (Ahmedabad: Navjivan Publishing House, 1982), p. 420.

2. Peter Nichols, *The Politics of the Vatican* (New York: Frederick A. Praeger, 1968), p. 199.

3. Gunther Lewy, *The Catholic Church and Nazi Germany* (New York: McGraw-Hill, 1965), p. 326.

4. As witnessed by church authorities "silencing" Leonardo Boff and "harassing" Gustavo Gutiérrez.

5. For one treatment, see John A. Coleman, S.J., *One Hundred Years of Catholic Social Teaching: Celebration and Challenge* (Maryknoll, N. Y.: Orbis Books, 1991).

6. For a contrast of proclamation and manifestation as, respectively, characteristically Protestant and Catholic see David Tracy, *The Analogical Imagination* (New York: Crossroad, 1981).

7. For Schillebeeckx's treatment of the *humanum* and contrast experiences,

consult his Christ book, the second in his famous Christological trilogy. In Dutch it is: *Gerectigheid en Liefde* (Baarn: Nilleson, 1984).

8. Gallup poll data indicates that American Protestants are much more likely than American Catholics to read the Bible either daily or weekly. See George Gallup, Jr., and Jim Castelli, *The People's Religion: American Faith in the 90's* (New York: Macmillan, 1989), p. 60.

9. See Nelle Slater, ed., *Tensions Between Discipleship and Citizenship* (New York: Pilgrim Press, 1989); for a profound sense of a deep reading of The Good Samaritan parable and a comparison with more superficial contemporary American readings, see chapter 6, "Along the Road," in Robert Wuthnow, *Acts of Compassion: Caring for Others and Helping Ourselves* (Princeton, N. J.: Princeton University Press, 1991).

10. David Tracy, "The Prophetic-Mystical Option," in his *Dialogue with the Other: The Inter-Religious Dialogue* (Louvain: Peeters Press, 1990), pp. 117-18.

11. See, besides his now-classic book, *We Drink from Our Own Wells*, Gutiérrez's reflections in Claude Geffré and Gustavo Gutiérrez, eds., *The Mystical and Political Dimensions of the Christian Faith*, Concilium 96 (1974). Jon Sobrino links his liberation Christology to the mysticism of the Ignatian spiritual exercises in a number of places, especially his *Christology at the Crossroads* (Maryknoll, N. Y.: Orbis Books, 1982).

12. The Jesuit motto reads: *ad majorem Dei gloriam.*

9

Lot's Wife

ELIE WIESEL

I chose this particular essay as an offering to my friend Bob Brown, for it deals with most of the social and theological issues that he has so profoundly and courageously confronted in his work. They are, as we are, linked to a theme and an imperative that brought us together: memory as ethos.

Only if we remember the other can our own identity remain redeemable. It is through the other that it is given to us to attain a higher dimension of humanity. We are who we are and what we are because of the other and our respect and compassion for the other.

Dear Bob: many words have been written and will be written to you and about you; yours will remain in all of them as a light that emanates warmth.

Let us read and reread the story of Lot's Wife (Gen. 19) as recorded in the text, shall we?

Two celestial beings, angels disguised as men, have come to bring good news to Abraham and Sarah: to inform them that, in spite of their advanced age, they will become parents.

On hearing their improbable, implausible prediction, Sarah, who in her youth was famous for her beauty as well as for her piety, burst out laughing—and then denied that she had laughed. Naturally, a family quarrel ensued. "You did laugh," her husband told her. "Why then pretend that you didn't?" Perhaps because they were embarrassed at having provoked a dispute, the angels left while looking toward Sodom.

"And they looked toward Sodom." What an ominous, disquieting sentence. It surely portends misfortune and evil. One feels in it a distant threat. Something serious, even terrible, will soon happen to Sodom—and Sodom is not aware of it. Even Abraham is in the dark. This is clearly indicated in the text. God asks: "Am I going to hide from Abraham what I am about to do?", meaning: the destruction He was about to inflict upon the most sinful of cities. Then suddenly, God decides to shift direction, to make a detour. He opens parentheses. Forgetting Sodom, He begins to speak about His closest friend and associate, Abraham: "Abraham will surely become a great, powerful nation; all others will be blessed in him. For I have chosen him to teach his children and theirs the path leading to Almighty God, to practice justice so as to allow God to fulfill the promises made to him. . . ." Then, suddenly, God closes the parentheses and comes back to the subject which seems to be at the forefront of His mind: "And the Almighty said: The outcry of Sodom and Gomorrah is mounting towards me. Enormous are their sins. Thus I shall go down and see for myself if the scandalous sounds below are true; if they are not, I shall know it."

And so we are plunged into the heart of the drama. Sodom is already lost, no doubt about it. The mechanism of its destruction has been set in motion; nothing can stop it; nothing will. Nothing? No. Not even Abraham's intercession. But . . . what about T'shuva? What about repentance and its extraordinary power? Is it too late for Sodom's citizens to mend their ways and be saved? Hasn't tradition told us again and again, since the beginning of history, that it is never too late for T'shuva, never too late to turn towards heaven and implore its forgiveness? Granted, it is not the angels' role but man's to awaken human beings and urge them to improve their behavior — but then, what about Abraham? Why didn't he rush to Sodom to sound the alarm? Rather than argue with God over the hypothetical number of Tzadikim, of Just Men, in Sodom, why didn't he share his knowledge of the impending catastrophe with its future victims? Furthermore, didn't he know from the outset that this debate was a waste of time? Can one win victories over God? The same question may be addressed to God, too: why did He allow Abraham to go on arguing, when He knew that there were no Just Men in Sodom? He could have said to His friend and ally: Really, Abraham, save your strength; it is of no use; it is too late. . . .

These are troubling questions. And we will explore them — later.

Often when writing or lecturing, I ask myself, What are we doing here together? My answer is always the same: we are trying to perfect the art of questioning. What is textual study, if not an effort to discover hidden meanings left to us by previous generations of teachers and their disciples? The Torah begins with a Bet, so we could ask: why not with an Aleph? In the Book of Books, the first question is asked not by man but by God: "Ayekha?" Adam, where are you? What is your place in the world? What have you done with your life? See: one little word, and so many questions. . . . Raised by God, they are all pertinent. Raised by man, they sometimes lead us astray. That is why certain "Sifrei khakirah," or books of philosophy, were forbidden reading in previous centuries. One had to be intellectually and religiously mature before studying Maimonides' *Guide for the Perplexed.* Were we that afraid of questions? No — not when they were preceded by answers. When a question brings me nearer to God, God is the answer. When it creates a distance between me and God, God is the question.

But, isn't God to be found in both the question *and* the answer? God wishes to be found inside, not outside. God is the key that opens all gates. Only human beings stay, at times, in front of closed doors.

Don't you think we ought to let them in?

Let us return to Sodom, that singular city where everything is expensive, except life and human dignity.

Is it dangerous to go there? Well, literature tells us that it is sometimes necessary if not fruitful to live dangerously. In Sodom, danger is selective: it only threatens foreigners. Never mind, let's go there anyway.

A fascinating spectacle has been prepared for us. A spectacle in five acts: the daily life in Sodom, the arrival of the three emissaries, the dialogue between Abraham and God, the destruction of the city, and the rescue of Lot. The pace of events is as breathless as the tale is devastating. At the end, everything will be reduced by fire; the most beautiful edifices will lie in ashes. Few managed to escape; fewer emerged unscathed. Lot and his family? Only some members of his family survived—his wife and their two unmarried daughters. Having survived an immense tragedy, they became its main characters. The others—for instance, the angels—played a secondary role.

Lot and his wife are at the center. May I publicly admit my sympathy for Mrs. Lot? Poor woman, she died the day she was liberated. First, she enjoys God's support in the form of a miracle, then she is deprived of the chance to reap its reward: she dies without experiencing the joy inherent in the act of liberation. She does not even have time to speak about it to her grandchildren. Why such harsh punishment? Only because she looked where it was forbidden to look? So what. If our own gaze could kill us, there would not be enough room for all the cemeteries on our planet. All right, she did disobey the angels' injunction, and did deserve a punishment—but why death? Wouldn't it have been enough for her to lose her sight? I feel sorry for Lot's good wife who arrived in the desert—to stay there forever: Josephus Flavius writes that he had seen her statue with his own eyes. . . .

Well—let her rest a bit, while we do what she shouldn't have done: while we look at her native town. Do not worry: at this point in our journey, Sodom is still intact. Flourishing—I mean: the evil was flourishing.

When we visit Sodom we realize that it is not only the scene of its collective tragedy which we are about to witness; we will also encounter one of its protagonists. Sodom has its own temperament, its own mentality, its own personality: all of its inhabitants, with some rare exceptions, think and behave the same way. One would say that Sodom is inhabited by one person alone, but copied and imitated a thousand times. The slogan "one for all and all for one" could apply to Sodom, with a minor change: all are like one and the one is selfish, violent, cruel, cynical, corrupt, almost inhuman. That is why God has decided to annihilate the city: its population had pushed its taste for sin, its thirst for injustice too far. Its people have caused too much harm to too many men and women. The Midrash is full of legends illustrating the moral depravation that reigned in that city which had become the world—or cosmic—capital of crime.

Look at the social picture: everybody was a thief, a liar, a swindler, a sadist, a narcissist, a monster. The people respected nothing and obeyed no one. They believed in no spiritual force and followed no ethical precept; they feared neither man nor their Creator. Nothing was sacred, and no one was safe in their eyes. Legend has it that once a year they gathered in a certain place to celebrate their right to free pleasure. How? Through orgies that the most fervent hedonists would find exaggerated and obscene: fathers slept with their daughters, husbands borrowed their friends' wives for one hour or one night—with the consent of their own wives—and all of this was carried out in public.

Still, their behavior towards strangers was worse: they saw in every stranger an enemy to be vanquished and robbed of his fortune and of his hope. One might say that they did everything to give tourism a bad name. To see Sodom meant to be exposed to ridicule, humiliation, and death—the worst, most violent kind of death.

A visitor who happened to enter Sodom could easily die of hunger: the inhabitants would sell him or even offer him anything ... but food. If he had food in his bag, they would torture him: they would make him lie in a bed that was either too big or too small. If it was too small, they would mutilate his body to fit the bed. If it was too big, they would pull him by the hands, by the feet, by all his limbs, deaf to his shrieks and laments.

That the Sodomites did that is bad enough. But then they pretended to torture the visitor for his own sake: to allow him to sleep more comfortably.

Worst of all, they pretended to act in accordance with the law of the land.

Whatever they undertook was ordered or, at least, approved by local courts. Strange as it may sound, there were four or five sitting judges in Sodom, says the Midrash. All had names that suited them perfectly. One was called man of deceit, the other man of falsehood, the third was head of liars. With judges such as these, the plaintiff never had a chance. He was condemned even before presenting his case, before opening his mouth. And Abraham's nephew, Lot, was ... their leader. The chief justice. But they listened to him only when he spoke their language and expressed their ideas; then they applauded him. But if he disagreed with their decisions, they interrupted him and shouted, "What! A foreigner came to dwell in our midst and he wants to rule over us?"

In other words, there was a system in Sodom. Air-tight and self-locked, it functioned with brutal and calculated efficiency. The system crushed any outsider who dared to challenge it. All trips to Sodom were one-way. It was possible to enter the city but not to leave it. Actually, according to one Midrashic source, it wasn't so easy to enter Sodom, as one might think. The Sodomites saw to it that all roads leading to their city were flooded.

Was it an expression of their xenophobia? or their idea of public relations? Did they think that if word got around that their city was inaccessible, more and more people would be attracted to it? Possibly. But there is a simpler explanation: since the ground of Sodom was made of pure gold, its citizens wanted all of the riches for themselves. Didn't they have enough? They did. But such is the nature of the selfish man: not only does he wish to be wealthy and happy, he needs to know that others are not.

If and when a foreign visitor did manage to enter the city, its inhabitants knew how to deal with him—legally: they assaulted him and deprived him of his possessions, but each person took only small things. Thus they could tell the judge, "Look, your honor, it's nothing. For this, I am to face charges?"

It was a game, nothing else. The Sodomites needed not fear justice. The courts existed only to condemn and punish the victim, be he or she one of their own tribe. Example: if a Sodomite struck his neighbor's pregnant wife who lost her baby in the process, her husband was told, "Give your wife to the man who hit her; he'll make her pregnant again." If a man wounded his fellow-man and made him bleed, the victim was told to pay his aggressor for the blood-letting.

Cruel to human beings? The Sodomites were equally cruel towards animals and birds—in other words, towards any living creature whose life and movement escaped their authority. And eventually, the Sodomites manifested cruelty towards one another. Yes—in spite of their plentiful natural resources, the Sodomites envied one another, were jealous of one another and stole from one another. Is that why God grew angry and said, "I have given you more than I gave others, and you use my blessings to make others suffer?" Is this why He chose to annihilate Sodom? We stumble here upon a serious and disturbing issue, that of collective guilt: does it exist within the framework of Jewish tradition? Could there be no innocent person within a community of sinners? Then what about the children, the infants? Are they, too, guilty? Guilty of what? Of having been born? Furthermore, even if guilt were all-pervasive, why were Lot and his wife and their children spared? Only because they were Abraham's relatives? Is nepotism a valid reason? If the answer is yes, why were Aaron's children punished by death?

Let's stay a moment with Lot—the permanent winner of Sodom's nicest citizen award. In the biblical text, he is introduced in flattering terms. Unlike his compatriots, he was kind and hospitable toward strangers. Is that why he deserved to survive? It seems so. Didn't he welcome the three celestial emissaries, even though he ignored their identity and was unaware of their mission? Both Scripture and its commentaries make much of this episode. He invited the three angels into his home, he offered them food and shelter, and when the Sodomites—all of them, young and old, rich and richer—came to besiege his house and demand that he hand them over, he refused: a perfect host, he protected his guests to the end. He went so far as to propose a deal to the aggressors: instead of his three visitors, he will give them his two young daughters, both virgins. "Do with them whatever your heart desires," Lot told the Sodomites. His plea fell on deaf ears. What they wanted was to sodomize and lynch the three foreigners; nothing less, nothing else would satisfy their vile instincts. They were about to break down the doors when, finally, the three angels—who until now were rather passive—decided to take action: they blinded the attackers and thus rendered them harmless. At this point, one feels like yelling, "Bravo, Lot. Well done. You are indeed special." But . . . wait. Let us not be too hasty. That the angels deserve our praise, that goes without saying: angels are by definition praiseworthy. But Lot? I mean, not the gracious host but the father? What kind of a father was he, ready to hand his own daughters over to a bloodthirsty and sex-thirsty mob? Did he even consult with his daughters?

Is it possible that they agreed to be sacrificed? One somewhat perverse theory maintains that that's what they subconsciously desired. The reason? They weren't that young any more. And they never knew the mysterious joys of physical love. It is a fact that, following their escape, they abused their father's fatigue and made use of his vigor while he remained asleep. All right. Suppose they were consenting adults when Lot offered them to the populace—does this necessarily exonerate him?

Admittedly, the angels were grateful. So much so that they revealed to him the true nature of their mission: the entire city was doomed. "Take your family," they told him. "Your sons, your daughters, their husbands, take them and flee, for this place will be destroyed." Lot took the warning seriously. Quickly, he ran to meet with his sons-in-law; he repeated the precise words he had heard from the angels, and urged them to pack and leave. In vain. They refused to believe him; they mocked him for his fears and ridiculed his visions of horror. In the meantime, the angels grew impatient and began pressing him to leave; time was running out. "Do not linger," they told Lot. "It's later than you think. Your sons-in-law refuse to join you, leave them behind. Take your wife and your two unmarried daughters, and come with us. Those who were unwilling or unable to hear your warning, those who refused to be saved, too bad for them." Growing more anxious by the minute, the angels led them out of town by hand. "Do not look back," they warned them. "To look back means instant death."

There we are shocked by the behavior of the angels. That they were in a hurry was understandable. But since they could perform miracles, why didn't they perform one last miracle and save all the members of Lot's family—even against their will?

And since we have come upon such a perplexing point, may we extend it to humbly ask our grandfather Abraham something about his own whereabouts during this phase of the tragedy? Where was he when his nephew fled Sodom? Granted, he argued with God and debated with Him point by point the unjust fate of the sinful city. Trying to save it, he bargained with God. His courage was evident, no doubt about that. But . . . why did he, all of a sudden, vanish from the stage? Let us read the text: at a certain point in the debate, Abraham gave up. He picked up his marbles, so to speak, and went home. *"Vayele'h adoshem kaasher kila ledaber el Avraham, ve-Avraham shav limkomo."* God having told Abraham that He accepts his challenge, and that Sodom will be saved if it had ten Just Men in its midst, Abraham returned to his dwelling place.

What is this? God was ready to annul His devastating decree if only Abraham could designate to Him ten Just Men—and Abraham didn't even try to locate them? to identify them? He didn't knock at doors, didn't consult friends and experts? He simply went home and did nothing? He, who knew how to fight, who loved to fight for his fellow man? What happened to him? What made him yield to passivity? What made him so resigned?

And, the question of questions whenever we confront someone else's tragedy, what about God in all this? How is one to explain His attitude? Before the destruction of Sodom, He seemed to play a game with His favored Jew—a game totally unfair to Abraham, who had no control over its outcome.

Clearly, Abraham bargained with God in good conscience. He couldn't have known whether there were ten or ten hundred Just Men in the city. But God knew! So why did He force Abraham to play such a ridiculous game? Why didn't He stop him right away and say: "Look, my dear fellow, do not waste your energy! It's no use! What is bound to happen will indeed happen! And there is nothing you can do about it." Why did He let him sink deeper and deeper into his own inevitable defeat? Is it possible, is it conceivable that God actually wanted to demonstrate to Abraham something that Abraham already knew, namely that the Creator is superior to His creation, that God's knowledge lies beyond that of man?

Admit it: All the protagonists here seem, at certain moments, determined to move us to dismay, as if to tell us, "Wait, you haven't seen everything yet. There are other surprises in store for you."

Lot's wife? Is she also going to surprise us? Yes, even she is full of surprises. We plan to question her—later. Do not worry: we know where to find her; she won't run away.

Let us retrace our steps and revisit the place of no return: Sodom. We had the usual yet doubtful pleasure of meeting its sinners. Was there really no honest citizen, no charitable woman, no decent individual in that entire city which was cursed by itself and punished by destiny? Wait: there was one. One person. One soul. A member of Lot's family. Himself? No. His wife? No. His daughter. We even know her name: Paltit. True, her name does not appear in Scripture, but she does play a rather significant role in the Midrash.

The Midrash offers us some interesting details about her personality. As the wife of an influential Sodomite, she lacked nothing, needed nothing to enjoy life and its blessings. Like the young Cakya Muni or Buddha, she must have thought that everybody under the sun was as happy and healthy as she was. Then, one day, she noticed a hungry beggar and couldn't help but feel sorry for him. Unfortunately, that was forbidden in Sodom, where human responses were declared illegal. So she brought him food under cover of night. At first, the Sodomites failed to understand how the beggar managed to survive. Eventually, they figured it out. Paltit was arrested. Tried. Judged. Sentenced to die at the stake. In her agony, she screamed to heaven: "Master of the Universe, be my judge and the Judge of Sodom." That is when God decided to leave His celestial throne and pass judgment upon her tormentors and executioners. This is suggested in the biblical text, *"Erda-na ve-ere ha-ketzakata habaa elai:* I must go down below and see what is happening, for her outcry has reached me." One outcry only? Or the outcry of a single woman? Indeed, it happened that the suffering inflicted upon one person moved God more than the pain endured by multitudes.

Does it mean that Paltit was the only Just Person in Sodom? There was another one, claims the Midrash, which tells the story of two girl friends who would go together to draw water from the fountain. "You look bad," said the one. The other did not answer. But the first one was so insistent that her friend had to explain, "We have no food at home." The first girl came from a wealthier family and could have helped her friend, but again, compassion was considered a crime in Sodom. The rich girl had an idea: she filled her jug with grain. The two friends exchanged jugs. The generous one also ended up on the stake. And it is because of her suffering that God destroyed Sodom.

Another Midrashic text describes another sinful town (there were five of them) where a nice young girl also felt sorry for a stranger. She too was arrested, judged, and sentenced to death: this time not by fire, but by the sting of thousands of bees. And it was because of her that Sodom was punished.

Thus the Midrash seems to emphasize the importance of individual suffering. I like such an attitude. I like to think that when a victim, any victim, feels pain, God listens. When a person, any person, is tortured, God is moved to bring justice. But . . . wait a minute: any person? any victim? God was unable to bear the pain of a charitable Sodomite girl. But what about the pain of the strangers who happened to visit Sodom? Am I to conclude that their tears left God indifferent? Does the agony of a Sodomite weigh more heavily upon God than that of the others? Does God practice discriminatory love towards victims of different ethnic groups?

Good questions? They prove that the divine meaning of human justice or injustice has often eluded its victims. This is true even to a higher degree for Lot's wife. She has been saved—correction: she was meant to be saved. Look at the list of the survivors; she is there. Why? Because Lot was her husband? Was she better than other wives in Sodom? The Midrashic answer is a resounding "no." She was no less wicked than her peers. If she became a pillar of salt, it was not because she looked back, but because of what she had done before. It was because of her that Lot's three celestial guests were discovered. Listen: upon their unexpected arrival, Lot turned to his wife and asked her to offer them the customary bread and salt. "Right away," she said. And went to knock at the door of her neighbors: could she please borrow some salt? They were curious: why did she need salt all of a sudden? "It's for our guests," she replied. That is how the inhabitants of Sodom learned of the presence of strangers in their midst. And since the punishment is usually meant to fit the crime, she turned into salt.

Let us stop again. We need respite from this tale of evil and misfortune. With the notable exception of two local girls, none of the protagonists seems irreproachable. Not even the supreme Judge? He could have issued earlier warnings to Sodom, telling its citizens of their impending fate; he could have incited them to repent. Did He? The Midrash says yes, He did. According to one source, many natural and unnatural catastrophes had struck Sodom during the fifty-two years preceding the biblical story. All of these upheavals, wars, and earthquakes were meant to awaken the Sodomites. A nice try, but there is no hint of this in the biblical text. Did God do nothing because He knew all along that Sodom would remain Sodom? But . . . haven't we learned from Rabbi Akiba that *"hakol tzafoui,* everything is foreseen on the human level, but on the level of God, everything is still possible?"

Do I appear to want to become Sodom's legal defender? Don't I realize that such efforts, however valiant and selfless they might be, would end in failure? If Abraham lost, how could I expect to win? Still, may I be allowed to have a closer look at the file? It seems to me that one question ought to dominate our tale: is collective punishment compatible with the Jewish tradition. Regrettably, the answer is yes. The Bible speaks of an *"Ir ha-nidah'at"* — a rebellious, sinful, isolated and doomed city which must, according to the Law, be annihilated. Totally. The law seems cruel? Yes, but . . . it is one of those laws that exist on the page but have never been implemented. Sodom's case is an exception, and what's more: it is predated, hence illegal? Abraham believes so. And doesn't hesitate to say it. For him, there is no collective punishment. Remember Abraham's celebrated out-burst: *"Hashofet kol haaretz lo yasse mishpat* — can you, the Judge of all that exists, commit an injustice?"* He continues: "Are you really going to punish, to kill the Just and the wicked together?" In other words, whether someone does good or evil will have no effect on your reaction? Does it mean that the Just may not be rewarded, worse: that he may be punished? for what? for being just? (By the way, the problem of theodicy is only half-articulated here. Usually, we protest the happiness of the wicked and the unhappiness of the Just; only the second part of the enigma is touched upon in this biblical passage.) What pains and shocks Abraham is that *all* people could be equal in the eyes of the Almighty. We understand Abraham's perplexity. If the wicked and the Just are equal, on any level, how is one to differentiate between them? Isn't Judaism a desire, a need to distinguish good from evil, the sacred from the profane?

And — what is God's answer to Abraham's objections? He simply states that there is no Just Man left in Sodom. In other words, "Do not worry, Abraham, nothing bad will happen to the Just; there are no Just Persons over there. If there were, I would save them. Better yet: I would save everybody else as well. . . . "

And so — the case may be closed. Everything is settled. Abraham has nothing to reproach himself for, nor does God. Abraham has done his duty. As has God. Could Abraham have pushed the debate a bit further? He could have said, "Please, God, save Sodom even if it is for the sake of a single Just citizen." But Abraham realized that it was pointless to continue. He had lost, and he knew it. That is why he picked himself up and went home. What else could he have done? At least, his close relatives would be saved. . . .

And yet . . . if Lot and his children were saved, Abraham could not take credit for it. Uncle Abraham didn't even mention them in his plea bargaining. It was God's idea, or His angels', not Abraham's. Aren't we entitled to ask: why wasn't it? In other words, why didn't Abraham intercede on their behalf? Is it that he suddenly understood that they too were sinners? Lot's wife too? and their children? But then, why were they worthy of being spared?

The Midrashic commentaries tend to be harsh towards the entire family. Not only was Lot part of Sodom's corrupt system, he was said to have been a sex maniac. Whatever he did, wherever he went, he looked for women. The verse "And Lot lifted his eyes and saw the entire Jordan valley" is interpreted by Rabbi Nahman bar Hanina in a purely erotic way. . . .

The other members of the family? Better not talk about them. Well, let's. Lot's wife? She betrayed the three guests. The children? Two daughters were married, the two others were not. When Lot told them of the impending catastrophe, his two sons-in-law snapped back at him, "Are you crazy? Poor Lot, do you really want to convince us that our city is on the edge of disaster? Don't you hear the music, the songs that come from its streets and houses? A city that sings is about to perish, is that what you are telling us?" And so — they stayed behind. And their wives too. And their children. The two sons-in-law were fools. After all, their father-in-law was not just anyone. He had access to important people. If he was panicking, they should have listened. Naturally, Lot should have insisted on their departure, but time *was* running out. The angels told him so. Every minute could have been the last. Soon flames would come down from heaven and . . .

Escorted by the angels, Lot and his wife and their two unmarried daughters fled the burning city. At that moment, the Midrashic tale dramatically changes course. Suddenly, the mother appears as a positive figure. Disobeying the angels' order, she looked back, and what she saw filled her with . . . with what? With fear, says one source: she saw the magnitude of the catastrophe and died. She was filled with light, claims another source: she saw the Shekhina with impunity.

(Incidentally, looking back was severely judged in antiquity. When Orpheus rescued Euridice from the land of the dead, he received a similar warning. Unable to resist his curiosity, he lost his beloved forever.)

But why did Lot's wife transgress this prohibition? The Midrashic explanation is charitable. It was her maternal instinct that made her look back. She wanted to see the place where she had left her two daughters behind. She was a mother, after all. A compassionate mother. Sodom had not hardened her heart. She continued to love her children and grandchildren. She loved them even more, knowing that they were dead: how could she have abandoned them without even looking at what was left of them?

The two surviving daughters? They were granted extenuating circumstances. Convinced that their immediate family represented the entire human species (as in the time of the Floods), they felt an obligation to perpetuate it. It's a normal impulse, isn't it? They did it with their father — so what? They had to leave *something* for future psychoanalysts. . . . Anyway, there were no other men around. And didn't Noah's daughters do the same thing with *their* father? Anyway, Lot's daughters may have felt like strangers to their father: didn't he treat them as strangers when he offered them to the mob that had besieged their house back in Sodom?

A Midrashic text goes even farther. It suggests that the two single daughters had no choice: they had to bear Lot's children so as to allow King David to be born — David, a descendant of Ruth the Moabite, who was herself a descendant of Lot's daughter. In other words: in this case, incest seemed necessary if not unavoidable. Without it, Jewish history would not have moved toward messianic redemption.

So all were rehabilitated — all? Almost all. Not Lot. He is a difficult case. As a character, he is not too appealing. Why did he flee Sodom in such haste? Once out of town, he didn't even look back. How can a father detach himself from his children with such ease? Granted, the angels ordered him not to look back — so what? Was he so pious that he couldn't disobey them? His wife seems more sensitive, more vulnerable, more human. Having lost, in one minute, all her belongings, having been separated from some of her children, she felt irresistibly drawn to them, she *had* to look back one last time before confronting the future. Frightened and tormented by a possible guilt feeling for having survived, she was looking for her two married daughters: where were they? Is it possible that, being unable to locate them, she *wanted* to stay behind, even as a statue? Had she been alive, would she have permitted the incestuous act? And what about her husband? Why did he permit it?

The only thing that Lot could say in his defense was that he was . . . drunk. Still, at least one text maintains that he wasn't *that* drunk while his daughters. . . . Lot? An egocentric hedonist: how could *he* be exonerated? Well, he was.

Listen to the next phase of the tale: when Lot escaped from the burning city, he made a request to the angels. On whose behalf? On behalf of unknown people. "Look," he told them. "Look at that little town; its name is Mitzar. I implore you: spare it from destruction. I want to go and find refuge there. Naturally, I could try the mountains, but I prefer cities. I prefer that city. Let it live." And, lo and behold, the angels heeded his plea.

Astonishing, isn't it? Lot succeeded where Abraham failed. He saved human lives. He saved an entire community. An entire city.

Thus, at last we find ourselves ready to be reconciled with Lot. And his daughters. And their mother.

But . . . what about Abraham? He taught us an important lesson: It is always good to argue. Even if the debate seems pointless, continue to fight. And . . . to bargain.

Well — it is time for us to leave Sodom. What is the meaning of its history? Victory or defeat? Or both perhaps? Ultimately, Sodom means the failure of a society, and the triumph of a few individuals. What was the Sodomite society guilty of? It condemned itself by rejecting and humiliating and oppressing the poor, the stranger, the refugee — who more than anything need compassion and generosity. The story of Sodom is the story of a warning to each of us for all time.

The lesson? A society that negates the humanity of its weaker human components is in fact bequeathing if not producing its own misfortune and malediction. Sodom is not only a place of long ago; its flames rushed through our recent past and tore its buildings apart.

In conclusion:

Our history is reflected in Lot's story. Questions about him apply to us as well. Must I articulate them? Why did my contemporaries in Europe refuse to believe that death was near? Why did so many children fall victim to so many murderers? Where was divine justice? Why did one survive while so many others did not? Why did my generation lack intercessors, while even Sodom did not? These questions are troubling, and they are eternal. The answers? I do not know them.

All I know is that I understand Lot's wife better than him. For at times one must look backwards — lest one run the risk of turning into a statue. Of stone?

No: of ice.

10

Bridging the Gap

Pain and Compassion

KAREN LEBACQZ

Oppression is a reality. It has therefore become acceptable to speak of oppressed and oppressors. I have done so myself.[1] Yet this language carries a danger: the danger of division, of widening the already too-wide gap between people. Oppressed and oppressors become enemies, standing in opposition. If the oppressed are given epistemological privilege, then groups will vie with each other for the status of oppressed. Who is to count as oppressed? Whose voices are to be privileged? Is there a way to bridge the gap and speak not as enemies or as stereotyped "oppressors" and "oppressed" but as humans sharing a common core?

I believe there is. Yet the task is not easy. There is a danger, too, in assuming too quickly a base from which we can speak across the divide. I have long been skeptical of the language of "solidarity with the oppressed." I think it is very difficult for any oppressor to stand in solidarity with those who are being oppressed. I was once asked if men could be feminists. I answered, "Yes, but only if you are willing to call yourself my sister." My interlocutor immediately drew back: He wanted to claim the title of feminist, but did not want to *identify* with women. To call himself my "sister" was language he could not honor; as a man it was repugnant to him to be identified with women. Yet how could he possibly stand in solidarity with women unless he could accept such identification?

This is the constant danger in trying to find common ground: oppressors want the common ground to be on *their* terms, not on terms set by the oppressed. Thus, for example, one claims that all people are oppressed, rich as well as poor. Such claims are in one sense true, since systems affect everyone. Yet such claims also mute the voices of protest from the poor and become a way for the wealthy to secure their own privilege once again by preempting the language of the oppressed.

Christians who would accept the challenge of prophetic Christianity must therefore avoid the Scylla of undue division between people and at the same time the Charybdis of false harmony. As one who experiences herself both as oppressor and as oppressed, I propose that there is a bridge between the two. The bridge is suffering. The only way to cross it is with compassion tempered by sensitivity to structural injustices.

Pain and Suffering

There is no way to live in this world as a human being without experiencing pain. All humans suffer.[2] As C. S. Song puts it, suffering "is the one place where all persons — kings, priests, paupers and prostitutes — recognize themselves as frail and transient human beings in need of God's saving love."[3] While it is true that most victims of sexual abuse are women, for example, it is also true that many men experience sexual abuse as children. Others experience physical abuse, or psychological abuse, or the pain of loss.

Even the most prototypical white, middle-class, Euro-American powerful male will, therefore, have his own history of pain. Many if not most men have had experiences of rejection, belittling, exclusion — experiences of harmful behaviors that are similar to those experienced by oppressed groups. While privileged men may suffer these experiences as individuals, not because of their identification with a particular disadvantaged group, nonetheless the pains of the experience are very real.

It is this core of suffering that provides the possibility for commonality among humans. If the suffering caused by hunger, want, exclusion, or denigration is terrible when it is experienced by oppressed people, then it is also terrible when it is experienced by any people. The color of one's skin, the configuration of one's genitals — these make no difference in the face of genuine pain and suffering. It is no wonder that the men's movement has surfaced in the last few years and that its cry is a cry for healing the pains of childhood. These pains are real, and to ignore them is to do men an injustice. At their best, men can use this pain from personal experience to begin to understand what it feels like for others to be excluded, denigrated, raped, beaten, robbed, ridiculed, and repressed. Pain or suffering, then, can be the beginning point for a bridge between oppressed and oppressor.

The Logic of Suffering: Compassion

But to honor suffering as a bridge between kings and paupers, priests and prostitutes is also to imply that we need new ways of thinking. Our logic cannot shut out the voice of pain, or it will shut us off from the very experiences that might help us to bridge the gap. Thus, a new logic is necessary. James Cone, Dorothee Soelle, Enrique Dussel — these are only a few of those from oppressed groups who have argued that we need new ways of thinking that honor our deeper experiences of feeling.[4] Objective, neutral, detached knowledge is not what is needed. What is needed is passion, the ability to *feel* and *suffer* one's experiences. Scholarship itself blocks our ability to know when it shuts out our deepest experiences of pain. What is most true is not necessarily what is most objective, detached, and dispassionate.

This new mode of thinking can be called compassionate thinking or compassionate knowing. Compassion, suffering with another, is the new logic demanded in order to bridge the gap between oppressed and oppressor. To have compassion is to move to relieve the other's pain. Thus, compassion is also the first step toward rectification of injustice.[5]

But what is it that moves us to have compassion, to want to relieve the pain of another? Hobbes thought pity (his word for compassion, though contemporary scholars would generally distinguish the two) was the "imagination" or "fiction" of future calamity to oneself.[6] In other words, what we feel for the other when we feel pity or compassion is not so much the other's pain as it is a projection of the imagined pain that we would feel if the misfortune of the other were to happen to us. Here, being in touch with one's own feelings and experiences of suffering would surely be an important foundation for such imagination or projection. The importance of feeling one's own suffering is that it allows us to imagine the sufferings of others and to react with compassion.

But some feminists have argued that compassion need not be projecting outward from one's own experience. Rather, it can be a simple act of "receiving" the other. Nel Noddings, for example, suggests that mothers feel the pain of their children directly.[7] Wendy Farley concurs: compassion is direct knowledge of the suffering of another — "authentic, direct apprehension of another's situation."[8] Drawing on the fact that the Hebrew term translated "compassion" is actually *rachamiem,* or movements of the womb,[9] feminists urge an immediacy to the ability to feel another's pain.

This feminist approach to compassion offers an important corrective to Hobbes's view. If compassion is projecting out from my own experience, then I always run the risk of being paternalistic and presuming that I know another's pains when in fact I am only projecting my own reactions. Compassion as projection from the oppressor to the oppressed runs the risk of paternalism, which only continues the power imbalance. But if compassion is receiving the other into myself, then there is less danger of paternalistic or imperialistic presumptions.

Nonetheless, Hobbes had a point. Perhaps what allows me to receive the other is precisely my ability to remember and touch my own locus of pain. A poem by Naris Basu makes the point simply:

> My mother knew my anguish
> As only mothers do;

pitying my misfortune
For she had lived it too.[10]

There is an ambiguity here. Basu suggests that mothers have a special knowledge, an immediate knowledge of the child's suffering. And yet, there is also the hint that the mother knows the child's anguish because "she had lived it, too"—that is, because she remembers her own similar pain. In short, the ability to project out and the ability to receive may not be separate movements. In either case, imagination and feeling are at the root of the new logic of compassion.

Social and Historical Analysis

But imagination and feeling, passion and involvement alone are not enough. One can feel outrage at another's pain but still misplace the blame for the pain. More than anything, liberation theologians, feminists, and others who speak for the oppressed urge a need for social and historical analysis. Such analysis keeps the pains of personal existence from being perceived as idiosyncratic.

Take, for example, the story of the rich young man who came to Jesus saying, "How shall I inherit the reign of God?" Jesus answered, "Sell all you have and give to the poor, and come and follow me." Jesus' response is a compassionate one; he takes pity on the man's distress and sincere desire for salvation. Yet Jesus' compassion is tempered by a realistic assessment of the impact of structures on our lives. He reached out to relieve the suffering of the rich young man. At the same time, he recognized that the suffering was grounded in structures of wealth and injustice. The suffering could not be relieved short of changing those structures. The young man turned away in sorrow, for he was very rich. As great as was his suffering, he was not ready to change the structures. Feeling pain is not alone enough to lead us to the reign of God. Changing structures is also necessary. If we use this biblical passage in the manner that Segundo calls "deutero-learning,"[11] or learning to learn, it tells us that direct response to the pains of another must always be attentive to the structures that define those pains.

Such attentiveness is necessary because our pains are not just personal pains borne out of the difficulties of childhood or the peculiarities of our teachers or parents. Our pains are structural pains: pains allowed by and built into systems. For example, in the United States, women of every color make less in every job category than do their male counterparts. Men of color make less than their white male counterparts.[12] Statistics indicate that low salary is not just an aberration or a manifestation of the private peculiarities of a person's life history. Low salaries are structured and systemic: if one is a person "of color" and/or female, one will make less than the typical white male in a similar job classification. It is these systemic patterns that render some people's sufferings *oppression* rather than simply misfortune.

While pain or suffering is the beginning of a link between oppressed and oppressor, then, it is important to look for the causes of pain and to see the historical, social, and cultural complex within which pain is experienced. The child who is sexually abused by her father or her brother or her uncle suffers the misfortunes of fate — of having this father, or that brother, or that uncle. But she also suffers from being female in a system in which women are degraded and used by men. She suffers not merely the misfortunes of fate but also the sins of injustice. Child abuse cannot be understood without attention to these structural problems.[13]

A full appreciation of another's suffering cannot end with empathic feeling. Sufferings have a social component, and this component must also be understood. All personal pains are connected with social, cultural, and political dimensions. Feminists have long claimed that "the personal is political." Personal distress has its political causes — it is rooted in social arrangements and cultural values. It is important, then, to link one's personal pains with the larger political question of history. "Why do I suffer?" must be seen as a question that demands a *political* response: in what way does the configuration of power in my society and culture and world contribute to my pain?

This political response makes possible the full movement of compassion. The fact that we all experience pain may help us to be moved by any pain shown by another. But the experience of compassion, the genuine ability to suffer with the other, depends also on our ability to see how her or his pains connect with our own history, with our culture and social systems. Compassion requires not merely that I experience the other's suffering but that I recognize how our common history has created that suffering. Compassion, then, requires justice.

The Prophetic Challenge

The challenge to Christians is to find a way to bridge the gap between the haves and have-nots, the sinners and the sinned against, the oppressors and the oppressed. That bridge is rooted in the common human experience of suffering or pain. Honoring one's own pain can allow one to recognize and receive the pain of another. That pain must then be analyzed in light of social structures and systemic injustices. Only when the bridge of compassion moves to include the justice of redress will oppressor and oppressed be able to move forward into the jubilee vision of new beginnings for all.

The challenge that we face is both epistemological and social. On the epistemological level, bridging the gap requires that we hear and honor the voice of pain in ourselves and in others. It requires that we receive the suffering of others. It requires that we connect that suffering with the social and cultural history that privileges some at the expense of others. This means learning a new logic.

On the social level, bridging the gap requires that we use this new knowledge to undo the unjust systems of the past and establish a future in which oppressor and oppressed can affirm their common humanity. This is the vision toward which the prophetic challenge of Christianity impels us.

Notes

1. Karen Lebacqz, *Justice in An Unjust World: Foundations for a Christian Approach to Justice* (Minneapolis, Minn.: Augsburg, 1987).

2. In this essay, I am using the words pain and suffering as though they are interchangeable.

3. C. S. Song, *The Compassionate God* (Maryknoll, N.Y.: Orbis Books, 1982), p. 115.

4. Cf. James Cone, *The Spirituals and the Blues* (New York: Seabury, 1972; Maryknoll, N.Y.: Orbis Books, 1991), p. 4; Dorothee Soelle, *The Strength of the Weak* (Philadelphia: Westminster, 1984), pp. 84-85; Enrique Dussel, *Ethics and the Theology of Liberation* (Maryknoll, N.Y.: Orbis Books, 1978), p. 176.

5. See Matthew Fox, *A Spirituality Named Compassion: And the Healing of the Global Village, Humpty Dumpty, and Us* (Minneapolis, Minn.: Winston Press, 1979).

6. See John Kemp, "Hobbes: His View of Man," in J. G. van der Bend, *Thomas Hobbes: His View of Man* (Amsterdam: Editions Rodopi B.V., 1982), p. 58.

7. Nel Noddings, *Caring: A Feminine Approach to Ethics and Moral Education* (Berkeley, Calif.: University of California, 1984), p. 30.

8. Wendy Farley, *Tragic Vision and Divine Compassion: A Contemporary Theodicy* (Philadelphia: Westminster, 1990), p. 71.

9. Marianne Katoppo, *Compassionate and Free: An Asian Woman's Theology* (Maryknoll, N.Y.: Orbis Books, 1981), p. 66.

10. This stanza is taken from a longer poem quoted in Chung Hyun Kung, *Struggle to Be the Sun Again* (Maryknoll, N.Y.: Orbis Books, 1990), pp. 36-37.

11. Juan Luis Segundo, *Liberation of Theology* (Maryknoll, N.Y.: Orbis Books, 1979), p. 121.

12. Jackie M. Smith, ed., *Women, Faith and Economic Justice* (Philadelphia: Westminster Press, 1985), p. 25.

13. See Joanne Carlson Brown and Carole R. Bohn, eds., *Christianity, Patriarchy, and Abuse: A Feminist Critique* (New York: Pilgrim Press, 1989).

11

A Letter from Quebec

GREGORY BAUM

Robert McAfee Brown is a great theologian in the prophetic tradition. As a theologian he has tried to uncover, as few others have, what God's option for the poor means for the North American Church. I have learned a great deal from him. I admire him as a religious thinker, and I am very fond of him as a human being. In an essay written by him a few years ago, he recalled with great generosity the decades we have known one another, beginning with our first encounter in New York City in the early sixties. I am tempted to reply to his essay by telling my own memories of the happy associations I have had with him and his wife, and more importantly perhaps, of the causes involving theory and practice that both of us have defended over the years.

At the same time, writing for this *Festschrift* gives a Canadian theologian now residing in Quebec the opportunity to share with his American colleagues the English translation of an interesting church document from Quebec that is not likely to be available to American readers. This is an opportunity I cannot resist. Since the document I want to present reflects the prophetic tradition and the theme of liberation, it will be of interest, I am sure, to Robert McAfee Brown, whom we honour in this volume.

On May 1, 1992, the Catholic bishops of Quebec published a Labour Day statement that reflected the perspective of the social justice network spread throughout the Quebec Church. While English-speaking North America tends to think of the first of May as a communist institution and celebrates Labour Day in September, Quebec society chose over twenty years ago to celebrate Labour Day on the first of May. Over the years the Quebec bishops, in conversation with the social justice network, have used this occasion to articulate the meaning of Catholic social teaching for their own society. These pastoral statements have often offered a radical critique of the existing economic order. The statement of May 1, 1992, *To Live in a Democratic Economy*, continues this tradition. The following is a slightly abbreviated version of the text in English translation:

1. At a time when recession continues to rage, inflicting its terrible consequences on individuals, the Social Affairs Committee of the Assembly of the Bishops of Quebec shares the feeling of anxiety that is sweeping through the population in respect of its economic future. Common sense has stirred up a profound malaise among the people telling them that the situation can no longer continue as it is.

2. What is most intolerable in the current economic order is how social and democratic rights are losing ground before what can only be described as the dictatorship of the marketplace. We are in fact witnessing a significant weakening of democratic powers to the advantage of economic powers. The marketplace is imposing its laws; it has become worldwide, espousing free trade, and is marked by fierce competition. Transnational companies use blackmail to impose conditions for setting up operations on our territory. They can decide at a moment's notice to close down a factory without taking into account the social consequences and without anyone being able to persuade them to reconsider their decision. Locally based businesses demand that the State put in place tax breaks and other measures which they deem necessary to remain competitive, while lowering standards and quality control to a minimum. Excessive deregulation tends to reduce democratic control over economic activity, by denying the State important levers for adjusting the marketplace and correcting its abuses. Big capital becomes disproportionately more powerful than labour, controlling not only the ownership of the means of production but also the power of money and of influence.

3. When the State is asked not to intervene in a situation marked by such inequality in the balance of forces, it is the very essence of democracy that is put into question, replacing it with the law of the jungle. Must such a state of affairs be allowed to persist without seeking better democratic control over the economy? Is the role of the State essentially limited to creating an environment that is favourable to the competitiveness of businesses? Who defines the global objectives in our society? Is it not time to realize that economic policies and strategies conceived independently of social and democratic rights cause incalculable damage to society, even if they succeed in temporarily stimulating growth? Social justice cannot be guaranteed by allowing the free play of market forces. Democratic process and authorities are needed to monitor the subordination of economic growth to the goals that a society gives itself.

4. Within a social order which most refuse to question, certain economic decision-makers are nevertheless seeking to rectify this or that functional problem, whether it concerns industrial development, job-training, health-care, etc. In doing so, they rely on mechanisms of consultation and collaboration that point out a certain form of democratic economy: representatives of different sectors participate in the study of questions and the search for solutions. There are endless commissions and task forces on economic

issues to enlighten the different levels of government. The reports from these bodies often contain analyses and recommendations that are very relevant. This is already one way of initiating democratic participation in the management of public affairs.

5. The results, however, are disappointing in many cases, when one considers the needs identified and raised. The powers that be do not readily allow questioning of their ways of thinking and of setting priorities. In seeking to overcome the limits found in simple forms of consultation, some economic actors more and more advocate collaboration. Governments no longer have tools that are effective enough to permit them to intervene alone in an increasingly complex economy, without the risk of creating more problems than are solved. In the prevailing climate of commercial warfare between competing national economies, the survival and expansion of business and employment opportunities, as well as the development of the regions, cannot be assured without the cooperation of all economic actors. The growing consensus on this point allows us to hope for a healthier social climate, capable of bringing about a new sharing of responsibilities in decision-making. Such a transformation in mentalities is encouraging. It calls all social partners to a vision that is larger than the mere defence of narrowly defined interests and it can launch anew the spirit of solidarity.

6. As currently practiced, collaboration has significant limitations. It is confined to specific issues, in times of crisis. . . . Consultation and collaboration, as currently practiced, are insufficient to achieve the objectives of a truly democratic economy. They generally take place between experts or professional corporations and leave the population as a whole with a feeling of powerlessness in the face of economic decisions whose consequences it must bear. Many of these decisions, however, involve the choice of a vision of society that would require broad debate at every level of society and in every sector. Such is the case for decisions regarding monetary, fiscal and budgetary policies, regarding employment policies and the development of the Far North, regarding employment policies and job-training, and regarding social programs and the costs tied to health-care and education.

7. One might object that management of public affairs requires administrative and technical expertise. This is, of course, true, but such know-how bears first and foremost upon the means and tools to arrive at certain goals. Debate, however, on ultimate goals is not sufficiently encouraged in our society. It is practically ruled out from the start in the name of the economic fatalism that currently rules our world, imposing upon it its inflexible laws of productivity and competitiveness. Fundamental social orientations are dictated by a set of circumstances that are erroneously identified with "reality" or with "the nature of things," without relying upon sufficiently informed conscience as to the goals to be pursued.

8. Without a debate that is sufficiently broad based and profound, economic growth becomes to all extent and purposes the absolute goal, whereas

it ought to be situated at the level of means, with a view to human development based on justice and solidarity.

9. A democratic economy does not just mean discussion and formulation of major collective goals. It is to be achieved on a smaller scale in different sectors, through negotiation and participation in decision-making. Beginning at school, young people can educate themselves in democracy if they are permitted to have a say in the decisions that affect them. In the work place, people can gain greater control over operations and how tasks are allocated. The knowledge of salaried employees can be called upon to improve the quality of products and services or to adopt new strategies of production. In electoral ridings, public authorities can encourage better democratic participation by organizing public debates, by calling upon neighbourhood councils and other representative groups, and by making their exercise of power more open. At the regional level, decentralization of economic decision-making can permit more effective reliance on local information in respect of needs and resources. Initiatives currently underway in the regions, aimed at promoting greater self-reliance, must be supported by every possible means.

10. Such debates would be a way to benefit from the experience and knowledge gathered in community networks, women's and youth groups, peace and environmental movements, civil liberties associations, and local initiatives of all kinds. For certain questions of special importance, these debates could lead to a direct form of democracy. In other cases, they could generate mobilization, coalitions, and resistance and lobbying groups. These interest groups must be acknowledged and encouraged, for without them citizens would be powerless to work effectively toward ultimate social and economic goals.

11. We are fortunate in being able to rely on a community spirit in Quebec that manifests itself, for example, in the cooperative movement, in solidarity and mutual-help groups, in popular movements and community groups. In particular, we need to invite Christians to exercise their right of speech in Church communities and organizations. The Church must strive to achieve greater coherence between its own practices and the social goals that it promotes with other social partners.

12. We ourselves will always strive for democracy. Its forms will always need to be redefined to take into account the complexity of issues and the means of implementation. Democracy is founded on the deeply rooted aspiration in human beings to be recognized in their dignity, to become responsible for their destiny and to establish relations with others based on something other than merely mercantile considerations. We are members of a human community, before being actors in the marketplace; we stand in solidarity as a people with a future, not just as a competitor; we are persons who are consciously free, before being producers and consumers. We must refuse to let ourselves be locked into a fatalism that condones a division of the world into "winners" and "losers." It always remains pos-

sible for humans to affect the course of events, whatever may be the real constraints that must be taken into account. This conviction rests on our vision of the person as being in the image of God, a subject who is free and responsible for his or her becoming.

13. In being close to people who were despised, such as lepers, publicans and sinners, in proclaiming in the Beatitudes an inversion in the dominant values of his time, in declaring the primacy of the person over the law, Jesus showed to what extent the place of each one in the community does not depend on performance, status or merit. Every person is of infinite value because he or she is a unique creature and child of God. Therein lies something to inspire our efforts to build a more truly democratic society.

In the context of Quebec society, the bishops' Labour Day statement is not an abstract, idealistic account of what ought to take place in the world. The statement addresses itself directly to issues that are hotly debated in Quebec. It can be read in a reformist and in a more radical way. If read in a reformist way, then the statement supports the persons and groups in Quebec that favour the neo-corporatism, successful in some European nations, which brings together in consultation and cooperation labour, management, government and the public. Quebecers believe that because of their tradition of solidarity and resistance against English-speaking North America, expressed economically in their cooperative tradition, capitalism takes on a more neo-corporatist, social democratic form in their society. They refer to this economy as "Quebec, Inc." Such a more democratic organization of capitalism is supported by a good many progressive voices in Quebec, including several important unions. The bishops' statement can be read as support for moving boldly and vigourously in this direction.

Yet there are critical Quebecers who argue that Quebec, Inc. is largely a myth. They say that capitalists use the language of consultation and cooperation to make the industries more efficient and more competitive, but that their concern is not the well-being of society but the accumulation of capital. These critics claim that the globalization of the economy beginning in the eighties has successfully undermined Quebec's culture of solidarity and resistance that might have modified the capitalist framework. Quebecers, the critics argue, have become individualists, like the majority of North Americans. In this situation, according to them, there is hope only in the efforts of popular groups to build an alternative economy.

In the poor neighbourhoods of the cities and the outlying regions of Quebec now largely de-industrialized, growing numbers of people work together in teams to improve the material and cultural conditions of their lives. They create small cooperative ventures for consumption, services and even production; they relearn forgotten skills and produce goods for their own use; they form organizations allowing them to exert pressure on the powerful to protect the ecology of their region or neighbourhood. What is unique in their cooperative ventures is that their aim is both material and cultural. In struggling to improve their material conditions, people become friends, escape depression, and discover in themselves resources for love and generosity. While this movement is unable to transform the existing capitalism, it offers to many people a new way of life and provides new cooperative experiences that may eventually lead to a more democratically organized, largely scaled economy.

With the help of the Catholic social justice networks, some of the Quebec bishops have involved themselves in this movement. A radical reading of the Labour Day statement reveals the support of the Church for the communal creativity occurring at the base in Quebec society.

12

The Current Prophetic Challenge to Liturgists

To Enact the Impossible

JANET R. WALTON

"Only those who cry out for the Jews may also sing Gregorian chants," said Dietrich Bonhoeffer, as he worked tirelessly to resist and subvert the Nazi plan to exterminate Jews. These words warrant repetition again and again in our time. Only those who cry out for the Haitians, Black South Africans, Peruvians, African-Americans, the systematically oppressed and battered — the list is endless — may also break bread and drink from the cup in memory of Jesus' invitation.

Clearly differences in circumstances shed light on interpretations, but the connection between the realities that shape our world and the public prayer of the church is a timeless concern. In a society that prizes being Number One at everything — from winning a ball game to winning a war — how can we know what it feels like never to have had a chance to develop potential, much less to have it recognized? In a society where news of world events is conveyed in 22 minutes ("You give us 22 minutes and we'll give you the world," as radio station WINS boasts), how can we imagine the impact of the deprivation of basic needs such as water, food, shelter? In a country where free election is ensured, how can we envision the despair of those who expect a manipulation of the processes that produces the choice of yet one more corrupt leader? In a world where news sells best when it relates to infidelity, how can we overcome apathy in order to structure systematic change?

Where people gather regularly to break bread and share the cup of salvation all over the world in the midst of the most comfortable as well as the most desperate circumstances, what does this ritual act mean? More importantly, does it matter?

What we know of early Christianity suggests that this action was a political one. Jesus' identification with bread and wine aligned his body and his blood with the bread of affliction and the cup of deliverance, symbols for Jews of liberation from enslavement. Christians understood that their eating and drinking demanded the same association. Where anyone was in need of deliverance, whether from the deprivation of food or land or from human degradation, this need for freedom was the concern of all. To share in the supper was to identify such a conviction. In Robert McAfee Brown's words, this eating together symbolizes "sacramental subversion." "The simple act of breaking bread at the Lord's Table empowers people to engage in the more complex act of breaking structures of oppression that perpetuate the lack of bread elsewhere."[1]

From what we can gather of the early Christians (and surely there were exceptions then, as there are today), to eat and drink in memory of Jesus was not disengaged from the ordinary needs of every human being. There was no comfortable separation. Today the connection between sacrament and human exigencies often is not so demanding. Those who cry out for justice share the same cup with those who do not. Does this access mean that the action itself has lost its effectiveness? Does it imply that its demands are different in our times?

What would it mean if the eating of every Shabbat and Eucharistic meal were understood as an identification with liberation? That to eat such bread was to connect with the pain of every afflicted person? That to drink from such a cup was to participate in deliverance? "The Lord's Supper," says Robert McAfee Brown, "is not meant to be the extraordinary meal but the ordinary one, the meal that is the model for all other meals."[2] From that meal every other meal has the power to be extraordinary.

Perhaps such a vision seems too ideal and impossible, but that, it seems to me, is the realm of liturgy: to enact the impossible in all manner of ways; to hear it, to demand it, to live into it.

To Enact the Impossible: To Hear It
— A Musical Example

Recently Union Theological Seminary sponsored a concert entitled "Heroes of Conscience" honoring Dietrich Bonhoeffer, Hans von Dohnanyi and other members of the German resistance who died for their support of Jews during the Nazi rule. The program featured a number of pieces and performers with connections to these events, but it was an unpredicted moment in the performance that is pertinent to this discussion. After the orchestra played "A Survivor from Warsaw" by Arnold Schoenberg, the chorus and soloists remained in place. With the barest of pauses, the orchestra immediately began the next piece, Beethoven's Overture to "Egmont," Op. 84. At its conclusion, Christoph von Dohnanyi, conductor, again without stopping, led a repetition of the last section of the Schoenberg, in which the chorus sings the *Shema Yisroel,* the command to love and honor God. (Hear, O Israel, the Lord our God the Lord is One. . . .) The audience was taken by surprise. It was a moment when music spoke its prophetic word. Music that recalled the story of a Dutch freedom fighter executed centuries earlier was enfolded by music that recalled the wrenching story of a survivor. The music of an ancient prayer sung as Jews were marched to their death, set to a haunting twelve-tone melody, contrasted with the lush harmonies of Beethoven. Two expressions of beauty uttered an invitation to what life requires when the pain of many rages.

To hear what life requires is what prophetic liturgy invites. It is a profound attention to the sounds that beckon us to believe in ourselves, in others, in God, regardless. It is response to sounds that require us to be responsible for one another, regardless; to sounds that stretch us to walk on, even when the outcome is unpredictable, regardless. Nathan Mitchell puts it this way, "The hearty gestures and symbols of the liturgy. . . . forever revolutionize all our relations with each other."[3]

The sounds of liturgy do not scream out. They, too, are heard often in the juxtapositions, the story of a hungry person wrapped around the story of Jesus feeding the five thousand, the plight of an unemployed mother heard in the context of a covenant promise that God's mercy endures forever, or the victim of racial injustice grappling with God's seeming disregard for human need, rightly questioning, "Where is God?"

To Enact the Impossible: Demand It
— An Imaginary Example

The sacred 11 o'clock hour on Sunday mornings could ring around the world as a moment of reckoning, if Christians demanded more of liturgy. What might it look like?

The community gathers in a large room. The space, used during other hours of the week for many other community needs, is set with a configuration of small tables. People gather around them. No music is heard as people come in. Rather, they catch up with one another. New persons among them are especially welcomed. There is an air of expectancy. Something will happen here.

A teenager (or a person whose value as a member of the community is often unnoticed) begins to speak, inviting the community to listen to the mix of texts, sounds, movements that follow. What is read represents a combination of scripture and contemporary readings (always something from the newspaper and a variety of other texts). Musical sound is interspersed in styles ranging from classical to rap. Then someone from the group focuses a question, perhaps with a brief exposition. The groups talk for a time, perhaps 15 minutes. The conversation is an opportunity for all to share the connection between what they have heard and the realities of their own stories. The prevailing assumption is that each one learns here from others. Forgiveness costs. Honesty is hard. Solidarity requires listening. Death is not the last word.

Returning to the larger group, there is time for prayer, time to make demands of God, of one another. This covenant is not a casual promise but an expression of partnership which demands care about intimate needs, respect for anger, and yearnings for systemic reorderings.

Now it's time for eating and drinking. The tables are laden with food, some for immediate consumption, some for dispersal. A leader invites the people to recall the stories of God's activity among them, from the earliest recorded ones to the present manifestations.[4] The small groups, for these moments, listen as one. The blessing of the food occurs through this sharing, with some traditionally familiar words and some improvised. Then the bread and wine is passed around. Conversation ensues about what needs to be done in this area by these people this week. The food that is left is collected for distribution to those who need it.

As in the beginning, a teenager among them brings the liturgy to a close with the reminder that we are empowered by this food and conversation to cry out with those who yearn for justice, to weep with those who weep, to love God, ourselves and one another and to dare to act when such boldness is required. These connections are our promises one to the other, God and us.

Making demands of one another and of God in our liturgies will change our lives. No more sedation or passivity at the 11 o'clock hour. The witness of Jesus prevails on us to be mindful of one another, to take care of one another. That care requires listening, often better done while sharing food. But our promise does not end there. It compels us to something more.

To Enact the Impossible: Live into It
— A Real Example

In 1976 Sydney and Robert McAfee Brown came to New York City once again, to take up residence and work at Union Theological Seminary. The offer was to both of them, to be codirectors of a new ecumenical program, one proclaimed to shape a "new" Union. It was an opportunity to embody a fresh form of leadership (an acknowledgment of a husband/wife team, not a husband with a wife-assistant) and to be involved in an education that included the world's story side by side with the Christian story. The marginated peoples of this world, the oppressed in our neighborhood, would teach us. They would occupy a place of honor in the curriculum, pervading the study of every subject.

It was a daring move. Who could imagine that a well established theological institution would be ready to embody such radical management and curricular changes? Some say that the church is the most conservative institution of them all, while others refute with convincing examples pointing to the church's leadership in the civil rights movement and its active resistance to the United States participation in the Vietnam war. But since a visit on a Sunday morning to most churches would seem to affirm the conservative stance, why should one imagine the place that trains church leaders to be any different? For one thing, prophetic voices and actions have dotted Union's history. It is a place where well-known faculty such as Dietrich Bonhoeffer and Reinhold Niebuhr have worked. The seminary's administration has stood behind the value of academic freedom for its faculty members, at significant cost to its institutional life. The case of Charles A. Briggs was a notable example, when the seminary was forced to sever its formal denominational connection with the Presbyterian Church. The seminary faculty voted to take a 5 percent decrease in their salaries in order to fund a position for Paul Tillich, then a refugee from Germany. It has a track record for involvement with international concerns.

Still, any vision of change always meets resistance. In the case of the Browns, resistance won. After three years they left, convinced that their dreams would not be realized at Union. But the story remains an example of living into the impossible that liturgy demands and undergirds. Without doubt the covenant that liturgy expresses sometimes requires the choice to risk physical death, but more often what it demands is less dramatic. It is in the regular day-to-day working out of our lives — speaking though silence is more comfortable, or acting when support is minimal or nonexistent — that most of us have an opportunity to live into what is impossible. It is the challenge to overthrow unjust models of work. It is the prodding and poking and insisting on changing comfortable yet oppressive patterns of learning, of running a business, or of living on this planet.

In this instance two people wanted to try what others deemed impossible. Their legacy remains.

A Final Example

At the conclusion of the Browns' time at Union, they planned a liturgy for the community. The chapel renovation forced us to gather in the refectory. It was a fitting place, since their dining room had been the scene of much of what the Browns had symbolized at Union. Food of all kinds was always available. Amazingly (or maybe not) there was always enough. Everyone was welcome, and judging from their constant stream of visitors, many knew it.

The leaders of this service were drawn from those who lived, literally or figuratively, in the Browns' apartment: a Japanese student, a ballet dancer, a Roman Catholic nun, two young men in refuge from the draft in South Africa, and Sydney and Bob Brown. They represented a motley variety of needs and life experiences — something one could count on at the Browns'. Much could be said about the liturgy itself, but the point of this example rests rather in something else.

In the earliest experiences of Christian liturgy, people continued to worship in the synagogue but also in homes around a table. However, very soon everything was taking place in homes. Then, within a few centuries, homes were replaced by long rectangular buildings which had housed public courts. The meal was less and less identifiable. Finally, eating and drinking became so unimportant that people had to be reminded to do it at least once a year. That's our inheritance as Christians.

The rich legacy of the Eucharist as symbolized in the celebration organized by the extended Brown family leaves some questions for us.

What if we reclaimed our early tradition, meeting again around tables in rooms used ordinarily for other community activities? What if we converted most of our church naves into dining rooms and shelters and spaces for community organizing? What if we were led in worship by *all* of us, including the teenager struggling to find her place in our world and the person who rarely is accorded the honor of human dignity due him? What if people came to worship expecting to be transformed and empowered by the experience? As Robert Hovda has said:

Where else [other than at Eucharist] in our society are all of us — not just a gnostic elite, but everyone — called to be social critics, called to extricate ourselves from the powers and principalities that claim to rule our daily lives in order to submit ourselves to the sole dominion of the God before whom all of us are equal? Where else are we all addressed and sprinkled and bowed to and incensed and touched and kissed and treated like somebody — all in the very same way? Where else are food and drink blessed . . . and broken, and poured out, so that everybody, everybody shares and shares alike?[5]

A revolution is needed in our churches, such a turning and returning that the ordinary (Eucharistic) meal would be linked inextricably with every other meal; such a revolution that all eating and drinking would require participation in the liberation of everyone; such a revolution that the impossible is demanded of God and of all of us.

Notes

1. Robert McAfee Brown, *Spirituality and Liberation: Overcoming the Great Fallacy* (Philadelphia: The Westminster Press, 1988), p. 94.
2. Ibid.
3. Nathan D. Mitchell, "The Amen Corner," *Worship* 66:2 (March 1992).
4. A version of this type of Eucharistic Prayer was led at Union Theological Seminary at different times by Tom F. Driver and Michael Mitchell.
5. From a memorial card for Robert Hovda.

Interlude

The Prophet-Motive; or,
The Need for a New Vocabulary

SAINT HERETICUS

As has been well-stated in the poem, "The Truth About Adam Smith," in *The McGuffey Reader*:

> In Adam's fall
> We sinnèd all.[1]

Ever since that cosmic reversal in the eighteenth century, our theological linguistic system has been, as we say in the trade, shot to hell.

As we search for a new theological vocabulary with which to rebuild, we can diminish our sense of loss by co-opting some of the language Adam Smith's disciples have made popular, and using it for our own ends. Herewith an initial try:

Surely the backbone of our faith is *the prophet-motive*, in which individuals, often in situations of peril, speak and act on behalf of the oppressed and make stern demands on the oppressors. Since the longevity of prophets is in inverse proportion to the truth of their message, the staying power of the prophet-motive is ensured only by the *GNP* (God's New Prophets) who providentially appear on the scene just when all seems to be lost.

To the degree that the churches take on even a few aspects of the prophet-motive, they begin to resemble a new kind of *transnational corporation* — one that tries to put the good of the entire human family above either individual or national gain. When adequate resources are available, such churches look beyond their immediate environs to what used to be called the "mission field," where their contributions are ruled by careful *distribution and allocation of resources* (sometimes confused with *flight of capital overseas*).

Even in the best (or worst) of times, however, prophets are usually in

106

After Mowing the Field, Heath.

Playing the Cello, Heath.

Listening to Music, Heath.

Cleaning the Picture Window, Heath.

Peek-a-Boo with Caitlin, Heath.

Sydney Telling Bob That He's Wrong about Something, Sea Ranch.

In the Study, Palo Alto.

Sunset, Heath.

Bob and Sydney Talking, Harriman Picnic.

short *supply, and demand* for their services is muted by those who fear that the presence of prophets will "divide the church," and possibly lead to *Marx-schism*. This is true even when they do no more than denounce hedonistic trends, so ably delineated by Friedrich A. Hayek in his little masterpiece, *The Road to Surfdom*.[2]

Sometimes the rigor of the prophetic message causes people to leave one denomination and look for another, taking their pledge cards with them (*free trade*), or even foregoing the making of any pledges at all (*free enterprise*). Such actions foster an unfortunate situation of *anti-trust*. If pledges dry up, many congregations find themselves living beyond their means in acts of *conspicuous consumption*.

As an occasional remedy for such embarrassments, two denominations (usually one large and one small) may agree to a "church union," the larger church taking de facto responsibility for the assets and liabilities of the more impecunious member, in what are called *leveraged buyouts*, or even, to use a neutrally descriptive phrase, *hostile takeovers*.

The theological underpinnings of the faith, however, (to move to safer ground), remain constant even as the linguistic attempts to describe the eternal verities undergo significant change. There is, fortunately, the reality of grace, when empowerment is given far beyond what is deserved—what from a human point of view might be called God's *deficit spending* with no assured return on the divine investment, but what from God's point of view must be characterized as a manifestation of *surplus value* available to an unlimited degree. By contrast, all schemes for human self-fulfillment are ultimately exposed as, quite literally, "worthless covenants" or *junk bonds*. As their inefficacy surfaces, junk bonds lose their appeal even to those previously determined to make a bundle, i.e., the *economic determinists*, a hardy but ultimately fallible breed, as recent population shifts in our prisons make clear.

Occasionally the more cosmic utterances of the past, such as "The wages of sin is death,"[3] are scaled down to more modest and more empirically verifiable proportions, such as, "The wages of General Motors are not enough to live on." As a result, *unions* (not to be confused with "church unions," see above) enter the struggle to provide *protectionism* for the *workers* being thus abused. Similar diminutions of linguistic power are evident when clamor for a *peace dividend* in the name of justice is fine-tuned into a *piece-dividend* in the name of greed, ensuring that only the folks at the top will derive any benefit.

We note a final and disconcerting trend. The creation of a new deity has begun through a process of reification—to borrow a single term from the camp of the enemy.[4]

When an anxious question is asked about what lies ahead, the answer is no longer (as it was in an earlier era), "Let us pray that God's will becomes clear," but rather, "We'll have to wait and see how *The Market* responds." The Market is occasionally characterized as "sluggish," more often as "volatile," and most of all as "unpredictable." Whatever words are used, it is clear that in our day The Market is (a) an entity entirely beyond human control, (b) exerting power in ways that may not conform to the wishes of those who believe in it, and (c) "letting its reign fall on the just and the unjust alike."[5]

Such an analysis serves only to underline the maxim from (was it Tertullian?) *Forum Deus est*, or, in the vulgar tongue, "The Market is God." A similar equation, but drawing on the modern science of the comparative study of religion, is the maxim from (was it George Bush?) that "Reaganomics [a now-extinct thought form] is Voodoo economics."[6]

In both examples we see a similar instinct at work that has survived throughout the history of religion — the instinct to attribute supernatural powers to a human mode of thought.

To deal with these, and all other issues, supply-side economists have given us a diagram called *The Laffer Curve*. But by the time we have mastered it, we hardly know whether to laffer cry.

Notes

1. "McGuffey" is now recognized by competent linguists to be a corrupt form of "McAfee."

2. Or, as it is sometimes rendered, *The Road to Serfdom*. Accuracy in transmitting enduring truths is always at the mercy of fallible human beings. An interesting example of this comes from Yorkshire. One of the great rules for success in the agrarian farm economy of the eighteenth and early nineteenth centuries was "Buy sheep and sell deer." But this was gradually transformed, by the oral tradition, into a law for *stockholders* in the late nineteenth and early twentieth centuries that went, "Buy cheap and sell dear."

3. Cf. Romans 6:23.

4. Cf. Marx, Karl, *Das Capital* (E.T. *Capital*), *passim*.

5. Matthew 5:45, adapted.

6. Yes, it *was* George Bush.

PART III

VARIETIES OF
PROPHETIC TEACHING

13

Excellence in the Service of Justice and Compassion

MARY JUDITH DUNBAR

As prophet, professor, and preacher, Bob Brown brings knowledge to bear on the discernment of contemporary events, helping us see the historically defining moments of crisis and opportunity, of *kairos*, in our midst. Among the many who have been given vision and strength by his clarity, and by the congruence of his words and deeds, are those of us who teach at universities and seminaries and who seek, in the tempest of contemporary social, economic, and political realities, to connect knowledge to a passion for the common good.

Two major temptations for those in the academy, faculty and students alike, temptations to which Bob Brown seldom succumbs, are to conceive of excellence in largely individualistic terms rather than also in social terms, and to remain remote from engagement in current critical issues, including issues of justice. One of the ways Bob Brown overcomes these false dichotomies of individual and social, objective and engaged, is by seeing, both in biblical story and in later literature, the personal and political challenge for the critical time at hand, then and now. Thus he relished my account of Jon Sobrino saying, in context of Sobrino's reflections on "North American Jesuit Education from a Third World Perspective" (at Santa Clara University, 24 July 1991): "Is it important to understand Shakespeare? Yes, in order to understand El Salvador." And in a subsequent conversation with me, Sobrino said: "We could turn that statement around. Is it important to understand El Salvador? Yes, in order to understand Shakespeare." Sobrino added: "It is not that everything has to be political. The aesthetic has value in itself. But if the aesthetic were to distance us from the realities of injustice, that would not be right."

Is it important to understand Shakespeare's *The Tempest*? Yes, and among the richly varied, complex reasons are the resonances between major

111

conflicts in the play and a question central to debates in the contemporary North American university, a question partly rooted in Greek thought but given fresh exploration by Renaissance Christian humanists and by Shakespeare: What ought to be the relation of individual excellence to social responsibility?

Contemporary thought, religious and secular, often connects excellence to the development of a person's own deepest individual potential. But I want to distinguish that lifelong process of individuation, to use Carl Jung's word, from the kind of individualism encouraged by the material success ethic. And I want to suggest that, if we take our cue from Shakespeare, we shall be prompted to shift from a competitive ethic to a cooperative one, and to connect excellence to the service of justice and compassion.

The very word *tempest*, as Renaissance dictionaries suggest, and as Shakespeare brilliantly uses it, implies a time both cataclysmic and opportune, a kairos. *The Tempest* also figures forth both political disruption and personal discord; the sea-storm is related both to the outer state of the commonwealth and to the inner rage beating in Prospero's mind. Shakespeare connects the larger social world — the microcosm — and the individual person — "a little world made cunningly," in Donne's phrase. Prospero newly remembers these connections when he owns his personal fault which led to his political overthrow as rightful Duke of Milan by his usurping brother Antonio. When he begins his story, Prospero speaks to his daughter Miranda of his former self as

> Prospero the prime duke, being so reputed
> In dignity, and for the liberal arts
> Without a parallel (I.ii.72-74).

But in the next breath, Prospero suggests where the distortion of his liberal education began:

> those being all my study,
> The government I cast upon my brother,
> And to my state grew stranger (75-77).

The first danger to which Shakespeare alerts his audience by Prospero's speech is that instead of combining his roles of mage and leader, scholar and duke, Prospero divorces them from one another. Shakespeare is not, by this critique, suggesting an anti-intellectual opposition of study to the "real" world. What I believe Shakespeare is suggesting springs from Renaissance Christian humanism. The contemplative life of the mind is given high value; but if, as Prospero was, a person is called to work in the world, Shakespeare suggests that the person's contemplative life must not be cut off from the active life, or it will put the common good in danger. Prospero has cast off responsibility and severed study from it.

The second danger is that Prospero's studies have themselves become hidden, obscure: Prospero says he was "transported / And rapt in secret studies" (I.ii.76-77). And Prospero admits a moment later that the very obscurity of his studies made people overestimate their worth — a phenomenon some of us find familiar.

The third danger of Prospero's failure to connect his library and his dukedom is that his sins of omission leave the field wide open for sins of commission by others:

> I thus neglecting worldly ends, all dedicated
> To closeness and the bettering of my mind
> With that which, but by being so retired,
> O'er prized all popular rate, in my false brother
> Awaked an evil nature . . . (I.ii.89-93).

His brother Antonio's evil tempts Prospero to a fourth and yet more dangerous abuse of his excellence in knowledge: to put it to destructive ends. The rage, the inner tempest inside Prospero, tempts him to become part of a spiral of violence. A partly right use of his knowledge, his art, and his power helps Prospero put those who usurped him and their fellows through a series of trials which do attempt to serve the end of justice. And those who have done violence to Prospero have the opportunity to learn from their punishment — an opportunity which brings some to change their hearts, and others to harden theirs. But at the same time that he in part engages his knowledge to good ends, Prospero is on the threshold of distorting justice to vengeance, thereby abusing his power. "At this hour," says Prospero, "Lies at my mercy all mine enemies" (IV.i.263-64).

The turning point of the play comes a moment later when Ariel prompts Prospero to exercise compassion. Contending with his internal tempest, Prospero makes the difficult choice:

> Though with their high wrongs I am struck to th' quick,
> Yet with my nobler reason 'gainst my fury
> Do I take part: the rarer action is
> In virtue than in vengeance . . . (V.i.25-28).

The word *virtue* here implies for Shakespeare, as for Montaigne ("Of Crueltie"), the difficult exercise of a rationally chosen good in the face of resistance, the enemy not only without but within (who, in Pogo's phrase, "is us"). Furthermore, in giving Prospero the word *virtue* in precisely this context, Shakespeare creates a rich synthesis of the classical virtue, or excellence, of magnanimity, and the Christian moral virtue of forgiveness. In the great speech which follows, in which Prospero renounces his "rough magic" (V.i.50), he does not renounce that excellence in knowledge appropriate to human enlightenment and action, but renounces the manipulation of material forces which perilously intertwines with his fantasies of power, tempting him to an inflated view of his art as equal to God's:

> . . . to the dread rattling thunder
> Have I given fire, and rifted Jove's stout oak
> With his own bolt; . . .
>   graves at my command
> Have wak'd their sleepers, op'd, and let 'em forth
> By my so potent Art (V.i.44-50).

In this speech, we catch a glimpse of Prospero's shadow side, his temptation to abuse power which makes him brother indeed to the over-reacher, Antonio. Yet in the crisis of choice, Prospero resists his Faustian temptation to turn his knowledge to destructive ends.

Prospero forgives Antonio, but there is no sign that Antonio (or his ally, Sebastian) repents. Prospero must face the problem that although he can bring about external conditions for change, he cannot force the heart or will of others to change. As he changes his robe of magic for the robe of Duke of Milan, taking up the social responsibility he had once severed from his learning, he returns to the daily struggle to govern his society—the struggle for justice—and to the related daily struggle to overcome his own temptation to abuse power—the struggle to act out of compassion.

Shakespeare, like Dante and Milton, knew that the Renaissance ideal of human excellence—the vision of god-like potential in the individual—could be subtly distorted. "Here you will see," responds Virgil to Dante the pilgrim at the gateway to hell, those "who have lost the good of the intellect." Losing this good, the knowledge of God, Milton's Satan lost paradise, a Satan whose rhetorical brilliance so beguiles some critics that they take him, at his own word, to be a hero. *Hero*: a term our recent national history has made some of us probe with irony. *Paradise Lost* tests the excellence of a hero: What ultimate end does brightness serve?

Renaissance visions of the human story set ringing in my mind complex themes and variations of our own story: the ways we abuse knowledge by disjoining excellence in it from the ends to which it is put; the ways we divorce the intellectual life from social responsibility; the ways we often use technology for environmentally destructive ends; the ways (as the recent riots in Los Angeles remind us) we contribute, passively or actively, by economic injustice, to the spiral of violence (in Dom Helder Camara's phrase), and thereby also risk losing the opportune time (kairos) to work for a more just and compassionate society.

Parker Palmer suggests that at the root of these symptoms of "the split mind" (my phrase is the title of a poem by Denise Levertov) is what he regards as the dominant model of knowledge we offer in the university: "objectivism," which has as its aim primarily the observation, manipulation, and control of external reality, and which separates the knower from the known (Palmer, p. 27). The result is a tendency to relegate ethics to the sphere of private preference and to split individual happiness from the common good — a split researched by Robert Bellah and his co-authors in *Habits of the Heart: Individualism and Commitment in American Life* (1985). Feminist thinkers have studied a related problem, suggesting that a tendency to conceive of the self primarily in terms of autonomy, rather than equally in terms of relationship, fails to balance an ethic of individual rights with an ethic of care for others (see Gilligan, pp. 19-23, and Cole and Coultrap-McQuin, p. 8).

To the extent that these limited models of knowledge, behavior, and selfhood are institutionalized in our teaching and learning, they reinforce the split between individual "acquisition" of professional skills (a banking model of education, as Paolo Freire defines it) and social concerns. This split characterized the United States undergraduates surveyed by the Carnegie Commission (in the late 1970s); the survey shows, as Palmer summarizes it, that students are

> darkly pessimistic about the future of their country and their world. They are, among other things, "fearful of the economy, pollution, crime, morals, energy, and nuclear war." But at the same time they are brightly optimistic about their personal futures. They believe that the knowledge they have gained through education — especially with the access it gives them to their professions — will enable them to carve out a niche of private safety and sanity in the midst of public calamity. (Palmer, p. 4)

"They believe," writes Palmer, "as I once did, that they can 'win' while everyone around them is losing" (p. 4). William Sloane Coffin, in the 1960s, when chaplain at Yale, prodded my generation to struggle, instead, for justice, with his unforgettable one-line critique of the success ethic: The one "who wins the rat race is still a rat." Or, to quote Jon Sobrino, "Never congratulate a millionaire" (Sobrino, Lecture).

A key issue, for Sobrino, is whether education will lead to the formation of a "heart of flesh or a heart of stone" (Sobrino, "North American Jesuit Education"). I thought, as he spoke: *That phrase illuminates the core of* King Lear. And the play faces us, in a very different cultural context, with conflicts also at the core of contemporary El Salvador (and the United States' relationship to its power structure): worlds full of cruelty, violence, abuses of power and of rhetoric, and of the complicity which empowers oppression, worlds where it can cost not less than everything to have the courage to fight for justice and to show radical compassion. Shakespeare, though not to be made a cultural idol, can be a rich resource for the present cultural critique and for the formation of "a heart of flesh." But how, in addition, can such hearts be formed and "clean eyes, to see things as they are" (Sobrino, ibid.)? Ignacio Ellacuría suggested that in addition to its concern with culture, knowledge, and intellect, the university must be concerned with "social reality—precisely because a university is inescapably a social force: it must transform and enlighten the society in which it lives." He thought the university must carry out this commitment "with the means uniquely at its disposal":

> We as an intellectual community must analyze causes; use imagination and creativity together to discover remedies; communicate to our constituencies a consciousness that inspires the freedom of self-determination; educate professionals with a conscience, who will be the immediate instruments of such a transformation; and continually hone an educational institution that is academically excellent and ethically oriented. (Sobrino, Ellacuría, et al., p. 149)

Ellacuría's vision can be compared to the "new humanism" Michael Buckley proposes for the university:

> It [the university] must focus not only upon liberating skills to be mastered as in the Middle Ages or upon human achievements [and subject-based disciplines] to be known and appreciated as in the Renaissance. It must move to the developed appreciation of the human person and to the human community precisely as such, to a disciplined sensitivity to the human life in its very ordinary or even wretched forms. The expansion and innovation in the humanities must be into a sense of human solidarity: . . . As we would never say that an indifference to beautiful poetry, to sound history, to a well-reasoned argument, to the advances of science are consonant with a liberal education, so must insensitivity to human pain and isolation from the international community with its pluralistic experiences and indifference to the great questions of economic justice and of pervasive exploitation mark a human being a savage, whatever the technical conquests in terms of literary skills and refined tastes (Buckley, p. 229).

Shakespeare, however problematic *The Tempest* may be with respect to Eurocentrism, would, I believe, agree with Buckley, for the greatest "savagery" in the play comes from the "civilized" courtiers Antonio and Sebastian.

Buckley's argument resonates with yet another: Bob Brown's, in *Spirituality and Liberation* (1988). Just as Buckley seeks to overcome the split within students who acquire "cultivated skills . . . but little educated sensitivity to what is the burden of great numbers of human beings," so Bob Brown seeks to overcome what he calls "the great fallacy," that dualism which divorces spirit from the things of this world. As so often, his analysis clarifies the way forward. By analogy to his argument, we can refuse to divorce intellectual inquiry from social responsibility, distinct disciplines from diverse, global perspectives, and excellence from justice and compassion.

Works Cited

Bellah, Robert N., Richard Madsen, William M. Sullivan, Ann Swidler, and Steven M. Tipton. *Habits of the Heart: Individualism and Commitment in American Life.* Berkeley: University of California Press, 1985.

Brown, Robert McAfee. *Spirituality and Liberation: Overcoming the Great Fallacy.* Louisville: Westminster Press, 1988.

Buckley, Michael. "The University and the Concern for Justice: Search for a New Humanism," *Thought* 57 (1982): 219-33.

Cole, Eve Browning, and Susan Coultrap-McQuin, eds. *Explorations in Feminist Ethics: Theory and Practice.* Bloomington, Ind.: Indiana University Press, 1992.

Freire, Paulo. *Pedagogy of the Oppressed.* Trans. Myra Bergman Ramos. New York: Herder, 1972.

Gilligan, Carol. *In a Different Voice: Psychological Theory and Women's Development.* Cambridge, Mass.: Harvard University Press, 1982.

Levertov, Denise. *Candles in Babylon.* New York: New Directions, 1982.

Palmer, Parker J. *To Know As We Are Known: A Spirituality of Education.* San Francisco: Harper, 1983.

Shakespeare, William. *The Tempest.* Ed. Stephen Orgel. The Oxford Shakespeare. Oxford: Oxford University Press, 1987.

Sobrino, Jon. "North American Jesuit Education from a Third World Perspective." Santa Clara University. Santa Clara, Calif., 24 July 1991.

———. Lecture to Pastoral Ministries course. Santa Clara University. Santa Clara, Calif., 29 July 1991.

Sobrino, Jon, Ignacio Ellacuría, et al. *Companions of Jesus: The Jesuit Martyrs of El Salvador.* Maryknoll, N.Y.: Orbis Books, 1990.

14

Prophetic Christianity and
a Liberal Education

JERRY IRISH

I am making the final revisions on this essay as Los Angeles reacts to the jury verdict in the Rodney King case. The anger and despair that poverty and injustice always breed are palpable, not just in the misguided violence, but in the anguish all people of good will are experiencing as they watch the inevitable results of political, economic, and legal systems that serve fewer and fewer people. The gap between rich and poor, powerful and powerless, in this City of Angels has been widening to the point of obscenity, leading some observers to liken Los Angeles to a third world oligarchy. There are lessons in that comparison.

As the academic dean of a residential liberal arts college at the eastern edge of Los Angeles County, I must question our role in a society that has lost its way. In doing so I have become convinced that prophetic Christianity, as it is understood and brought to expression in the work of Robert McAfee Brown, offers a prescription for liberal education. Brown's biblical perspective reinforces the intellectual freedom and moral responsibility that characterize liberal education at its best. His theology in a new key is a pedagogy for our times.

A Biblical Perspective

Brown's juxtaposition of a biblical perspective to the acquisition of an undergraduate education highlights four dimensions I would expect to be present in a liberal education that prepares students for lives of personal fulfillment and social responsibility in a global context.[1] First, a biblical perspective offers us *an attitude toward the world.* The Bible, with its mythological cosmology, is not in competition with the biological and physical sciences for the most accurate description of empirical phenomena. To the contrary, it is often the biblical attitude of awe and wonder at the world that motivates scientific exploration. The recognition of our human contingency and interdependency and our sense of reverence as we ponder what may transcend the immensity of space and the fleetingness of time are other elements in a biblical attitude that fosters an open educational process. Second, a related dimension is the seriousness with which the biblical perspective takes the world. The search for meaning and understanding goes on *within the world,* and it is in this mundane context that human history has its fulfillment.

The third relevant dimension of a biblical perspective is *accountability.* It is not enough to have an attitude of awe toward the world and find our meaning there. "We are also enjoined to act responsibly by aligning ourselves with the purposes of the creator, and by working against those who thwart the purposes of the creator."[2] A liberal education should subject "the purposes of the creator" to lively debate, and one should be held intellectually accountable for one's views. But, one should also *act* responsibly. The biblical notion of accountability equates knowledge and obedience.

The fourth and final dimension follows directly from the third. "Knowledge of God and of God's world will be *transforming knowledge,* engaged knowledge, rather than detached knowledge."[3] Knowledge coupled with accountability is knowledge that makes a difference. In the story of the Good Samaritan (Luke 10:25-37), Jesus takes a lawyer's abstract question, "Who is my neighbor?", turns it into a concrete question, and sends it back to the questioner. "Who among them [priest, Levite, Samaritan] proved neighbor to the man who fell among thieves?" To the lawyer's correct answer Jesus responds: "Go and do likewise." The transforming knowledge associated with a biblical perspective is personal knowledge. The one who seeks to know is challenged to act. And it is in the acting that one really comes to know and is transformed.

Accountability and transforming knowledge make many academicians nervous. Is it our task to engender moral responsibility? Should the search for knowledge result in transformation or simply acquaint us with the truth for truth's sake? Brown explores these questions with respect to religious studies and concludes that there is no neutral stance. Indeed, the very scholars who deny any coupling of knowledge and personal engagement do so with great passion. And we see numerous instances of personal commitment elsewhere in the academy. In the teaching of Chaucer, or physics, or political science, scholars *do* take sides on important issues, and their debates enrich the intellectual environment. It is those who teach from a stance of professed neutrality that are most likely to smuggle in unacknowledged value judgments. Faculty members are well advised to admit the impossibility of complete disinterestedness and share with their students their own commitments and biases. There are no facts without interpretation, and interpretation is always from a point of view.

Brown uses the story of Jesus' two followers who are joined by a stranger as they walk to Emmaus after the crucifixion (Luke 24:13-35) to suggest how the educational venture might proceed from a biblical perspective. The process is a four-stage progression from *"seeking* the truth to *hearing* the truth to *enacting* the truth to *sharing* the truth."[4] The first and fundamental question the disciples are asking is, "What is going on?" How can any sense be made of the events that have taken place over the past week in Jerusalem, events that have left them walking away from the city, their hopes dashed?

For some time the stranger simply listens. Finally, he begins to reflect on what Moses and the prophets had spoken, saying, in effect, "If you want to understand what is going on now, you will have to ask 'What went on before?' " To understand the present you will have to draw upon the past, your heritage, and what it was that led you to Jerusalem and fed the hopes that now seem unfulfilled.

Despite the stranger's observations, the reconciliation, the compassion, the justice Jesus was to have unleashed remain empty concepts as the disciples enter the village of Emmaus. The stranger is about to go on when his peripatetic companions invite him to have supper with them. It is in this act of compassion that the disciples recognize Jesus. As they sit together at the table, he is known to them in the breaking of bread. In these deeds of the disciples and the stranger, enunciated truth becomes enacted truth, information about the past is transformed into a relationship in the present. Only then do the disciples grasp what happened on their way to Emmaus. "Did not our hearts burn within us while he talked to us on the road, while he opened for us the Scriptures?"

There is one more stage in this educational process understood from a biblical perspective. Jesus vanishes and the disciples head back to Jerusalem to tell the others what has happened. The learning situation is not complete until something has been done, until the enacted truth—the new relationship—has been given expression.

Truth sought and heard is more characteristic of our educational institutions than truth enacted and shared. However, pedagogical research is increasingly indicative of the essential significance of stages three and four in effective teaching. Nowhere is this more evident than in science education, where collaborative laboratory learning involves doing science in a team environment and then presenting to others the results and their significance. This is rapidly becoming the paradigm for education in the social sciences and the humanities. Educators who do not share Brown's biblical perspective might, nonetheless, agree with him that: "unless our treatments of our subject matter move us beyond the first two stages, making clear to our students and to ourselves that enactment and sharing are part of what it means to confront the truth, then I think we can ask ourselves how full has been our grasp of the truth."[5]

Prophetic Christianity

Brown's biblical perspective sets high standards for liberal education, standards consistent with the mission of residential liberal arts colleges and universities in the United States. His prophetic Christianity challenges us to reconsider precisely *how* we enable our students to think freely and responsibly in the new century. *Theology in a New Key* lays out what Brown calls "characteristics of 'the view from below'."[6] These "characteristics" constitute a pedagogy for our times.

"The view from below" is the description of a new perspective and is derived from a statement in Dietrich Bonhoeffer's *Letters and Papers from Prison.*

> There remains an experience of incomparable value. We have for once learnt to see the great events of world history from below, from the perspective of the outcast, the suspects, the maltreated, the powerless, the oppressed, the reviled — in short, from the perspective of those who suffer.[7]

"The view from below" refers to a lived perspective and presumes an existential shift in perception. Bonhoeffer's imprisonment and the perception of the plight of others it engendered came together with his biblical perspective and resulted in a new standpoint. In Brown's appropriation of Bonhoeffer's view from below, engaged transforming knowledge, the enacted truth of the Emmaus Road story, is wedded to a specific starting point, the poor.

Theology in a new key *starts with the poor.* It asserts an "epistemological privilege" for the poor, a capacity to see the world more nearly as it is, more accurately than is possible from the vantage point of wealth and power. In starting with the poor, in recognizing the extent of hunger and the incredible inequity in the distribution of essential resources, we come to the conclusion that the world should not be the way it is. Had the wealthy and powerful in Los Angeles looked at the world from the perspective of the poor, might they have tried to alter the environment that spawned the Rodney King beating and its tragic aftermath?

For prophetic Christianity, starting with the poor is not simply a sociological strategy. It is also a theological commitment, a claim that God is to be found at work in the life and situation of the poor. In the Hebrew Bible, God sides with the poor, and in the New Testament, God is revealed in a working-class Jew who casts his lot with the poor.

Educators can debate the "epistemological privilege" of the poor. But certainly we cannot quarrel with the pedagogical point that taking the position of the other is always instructive. In fact, it is absolutely necessary if we are to understand the claims made upon the traditional undergraduate curriculum by women, African-Americans, Latinos, Asian-Americans, and other marginalized groups. Until recently, those of us who are white, North American, and male assumed that only our chronological age distinguished our perspective from that of our students. That assumption began to be tested with the increasing number of women in our classes and on our faculties. It is certainly challenged now by the growing presence of students of color. If we are serious about being effective teachers, we must take the position of the other.

A number of residential liberal arts colleges and universities, my own included, have taken pride in need-blind admission policies. We enroll students to our high-priced, labor-intensive institutions regardless of economic means. But I fear we have also been "regardless" of what our students coming out of poverty could contribute to *our* education from *their* point of view. Have we assumed that it is in the best interests of such students that they shed their perspective and take up our own?

Theology in a new key *responds to the questions of the nonperson.* If one moves to the standpoint of the poor and other marginalized groups, one must listen to their stories and try to hear their questions. Theologians are used to responding to the cultured skeptic who wonders how we can believe in God in an age of science. While most college professors have not had to respond to theological skepticism, they have assumed the same affluent, white, male, North American framework within which such questions are understood to be appropriate. But increasingly questions are coming from people who stand outside that framework, people who have been crushed by their social circumstances and whose personal identity has been repeatedly denied.

The halting movement to inclusive language in the academy reveals the difficulty with which men hear their women colleagues and students speak out of their nonpersonhood. Like the "boys will be boys" response to the quest for security against acquaintance rape, exclusive language turns a deaf ear to the female nonperson.

As long as persons of color were in relatively small numbers on our campuses, their personhood was understood in terms of the degree to which they adjusted to a white environment. We took seriously the personalities we expected to encounter from our white vantage point. Now persons of color are present in such numbers that we must admit to not knowing very much about them at all. This is readily apparent with respect to the Asian-American student population, where differences in national heritage and number of generations in the United States have major implications.

The world in which the nonperson raises questions has become our world, as well. The nonperson's query can no longer be heard as "What must I learn in order to enter your community?" The actual question is, "What must we each learn in order to enter one another's communities and create a new community that includes each of us?" In the Los Angeles basin, our fabled multiculturalism includes hundreds of thousands of residents whose cries of desperation have gone without response. The Rodney King beating with all that followed in its wake is not just an African-American issue or a police issue or an issue for the urban poor, it is everyone's issue. A liberal education has to prepare young men and women to live in a community of differences. The best preparation is to practice that living on our campuses.

Theology in a new key *works with a different set of tools.* Given a starting point among the poor rather than the privileged, given the need to respond to the nonperson rather than the nonbeliever, prophetic Christianity turns to the social sciences rather than philosophy for its descriptive and analytical tools. A liberal education should turn there as well, certainly not to the exclusion of the humanities, arts, and natural sciences, but as an absolutely necessary preparation for responsible citizenship.

That the political, economic, and legal systems of the Los Angeles basin, not to mention the nation, are adequately serving a rapidly decreasing percentage of the population can no longer be a matter of serious debate. What is a matter of serious debate and, I submit, a vital subject for undergraduate teaching and research, is the nature of those systems, the reasons for their failure, and the possible remedies. It is hard to imagine a more meaningful and effective way to organize one's undergraduate education than to choose courses, select an internship, and write a senior thesis with the intent to answer a question such as, "Why do half the residents of a neighboring city live below the poverty line?" or "What are the causes and costs of teenage pregnancy in two or three nearby high schools?"

Theology in a new key *offers a different analysis.* The view from below reveals a world of conflict, a world in which major forces are polarized. Brown focuses on the polarity between oppressors and oppressed, noting that, though such roles may change from one situation to another, "those who scorn the polarity as mere rhetoric usually turn out to be comfortably situated, whereas those who affirm its descriptive truth are usually those who can easily discern the individuals and groups who are oppressing them."[8] The oppressed are in a state of economic, political, and cultural dependency which perpetuates injustice and thereby forces people to take sides. Brown argues that there is no neutrality with respect to conflict understood in this manner, and whether one stands among the oppressed or the oppressors, one is dehumanized.

As our campuses become more diverse, conflict understood in Brown's terms will certainly become more evident. Many of us who have held faculty and administrative positions in residential liberal arts colleges and universities champion conflict-free communities, and we accuse our women and minority colleagues of being disruptive when they are present in more than token numbers. We had taken the previous situation to be harmonious, because we had been the beneficiaries of an oppressive environment. But now the poor, the huddled masses yearning to be free, have followed Liberty's torch through the golden door and onto our campuses in sufficient number to make a difference. The hysterical accusations of political correctness coming from a number of academicians have more to do with the erosion of their unquestionable power than the reorganization of their curricula.

It is instructive for students and faculty alike to explore the presence of conflict, covert as well as overt, within their own educational institutions. Endowment investments and the exercise of proxy options have been the subject of considerable research and debate, as have been various forms of student and faculty governance. The discussion of free speech and harassment issues is revealing, and in some cases obscuring, conflict that runs not only along gender, race, class, religion, and sexual preference lines, but also across trustee, administrator, faculty, student, staff, custodial, and maintenance constituencies. Local zoning ordinances, taxation, financial aid, drug and alcohol policies, and handicapped access are all matters rich with educational opportunities, if the conflicts they express or mask are acknowledged and subjected to rigorous analysis. Colleges and universities are neither unique in being participants in the oppressor-oppressed polarity nor in exhibiting that polarity internally. They *are* unique in their dedication to the fullest possible examination of such matters within ground rules that protect honest and reasonable disagreement.

Theology in a new key thrives on *a different mode of engagement.* Praxis, as Brown describes this mode of engagement, is "the circular traffic that is always going on between action and theory."[9] Theology in a new key issues from engagement and leads back into engagement. It is rooted in the biblical perspective we have already examined and, consistent with that perspective, it is transforming. A liberal education that started with the poor, that sought to hear and respond to the questions of nonpersons, a liberal education that made use of the social sciences to examine the disparities that foster conflict, might also be transforming.

To link the dimensions of a biblical perspective with the view from below and initiate our seeking, hearing, enacting, and sharing with the poor is at once educationally sound and socially responsible. We might proceed in such fashion, not necessarily out of any religious motivation, but simply because the reigning educational methodologies are seriously flawed. For all the economic data we gather and analyze, for all the political science courses we teach, our economy and our political institutions are increasingly dysfunctional. For all the great literature we deconstruct or reconstruct, for all the philosophical arguments and world religions our students digest, provincialism and greed expand in those high places inhabited by our college and university graduates. Why *not* take a different approach?

Theology in a new key *is the second act.* It is reflection on the personal decision to be available to God for the transformation of the world on behalf of and alongside the poor.[10] The residential liberal arts colleges and universities I have in mind in this essay cannot assume the same faith commitment, the same "first act," on which to reflect. But we can assume our own version of the resources Brown finds available to theology. To a *situation* increasingly polarized between rich and poor, we bring a *commitment* to seek the truth about one another. Our multicultural *heritage* is rich with insight into the human condition and the opportunities we have to turn our campuses into *communities,* bodies of faculty and staff members, administrators and students, actively engaged in transforming the world on which we reflect together.

Notes

1. Robert McAfee Brown, "The Boundary Area Between Biblical Perspectives and Religious Studies," *The NICM Journal* (Summer 1981): 69-82.
2. Ibid., p. 71.
3. Ibid.
4. Ibid., p. 80.
5. Ibid.
6. Robert McAfree Brown, *Theology in a New Key* (Philadelphia: Westminster Press, 1978), pp. 50-74.
7. Dietrich Bonhoeffer, *Letters and Papers from Prison* (New York: Macmillan, 1972), p. 17.
8. Brown, *Theology in a New Key,* p. 68.
9. Ibid., p. 71.
10. Ibid., p. 73.

15

Deep Learning for Earthquake Country

PIA MORIARTY

All real living is meeting.
—Martin Buber

The vocation of a teacher of adults is to meet people who want to change. Immediately, the process is painful, because for fully formed adults to move beyond their hard-won status quo means inescapable loss and dislocation. Mature people know too well that something dies as something new is being born; this makes adult learning a serious adventure. The teacher accompanies these risk takers, which is a risk in itself.

Education for adults is not child's play, even particularly consequential or formative child's play. Such an assertion goes against the grain of mainstream schooling in the United States, where we prefer to project our needs for change onto the next generation. We hope and trust that little children will be more free to make serious social reforms such as racial integration. In our schools for training children, we have become accustomed to an education that is a holding and blessing operation. We hold students of a certain age in a certain stylized place for an agreed-upon period of time and then certify that they have been educated. Where learning comes into this process is unclear and increasingly unreliable to predict. Education has become alternatively social management and entertainment—literal or figurative television watching that keeps people in place, covers the material, and also develops intellectual couch potatoes.

In this essay, I want to talk about the dynamics of an *adult* educational process that engages the teacher with people who are intent upon changing their lives. These are adult learners who must move beyond the status quo because in some real sense it is killing them. These are dangerous people. As they move themselves away from oppressive circumstances, they will also move their more comfortably situated teachers into contact with realities that had been effectively avoided. Church traditions have words for this movement—*conversion, liberation.* In an educational context, I call it *deep learning.*

What I have to say here comes out of experience during the 1980s working in church communities on social justice issues, especially peacemaking, women's equality, and refugee concerns. I am based in California, which is earthquake country. My culture and belief tradition is Catholic, which has its own earthquakes and fault lines. In this article, I will draw primarily upon examples from my work with the Commission on Social Justice in the Archdiocese of San Francisco. That base in church community has afforded me the continuity of people and place and tradition that is stable enough to make apparent the necessary movement of conversion. I speak as a teacher to other teachers who work with adults reaching for social change.

Making the New Out of the Old

Deep learning involves the whole body, blood and bone. It cannot confine itself to theoretical consciousness raising or cataloging of insightful facts and analyses. In deep learning the mind moves the feet to walk in a new way, moves the eyes to see from the new perspective won by that walking, and moves the hands to fashion the tangible world into a new image envisioned by the new seeing. Deep learning takes what Paulo Freire calls praxis, the constant embedding of knowing and doing, action and reflection. Deep learning is cultural in that it involves the processes by which people make their lives together. It calls for a cultural artistry that continuously creates new living situations out of the old ones when they strangle life.

Deep learning is tough to institutionalize. Its process is too intensely disruptive and creative. Because it happens in groups, not only within the individual person, deep learning has the potential mass to make for social rumbles and shifts and earthquakes. It challenges people to begin working together to fashion a new reality *now,* as part of their shared learning process, rather than as a later, personal by-product. Some disruption is inevitable, because adult learners already have adult, engaged lives. We are attached to the way things are, even when that may be problematic for us. We are caught like the psychiatric patient in Woody Allen's story, who complains that his brother thinks he's a chicken but can't manage to tell him otherwise because the family still needs the eggs. It is precisely the life-threatening aspects of their established lives that people need to change. The question is how to sort these out from the basic values and dreams that make life worth living.

Deep learning takes into account those experiential themes and binds that are characteristic of adulthood. For example:

—need for respect from self and peers
—deep ties to a formative history

—responsibility to support the lives of others beyond oneself
—need to prioritize and balance obligations
—ability to envision and accomplish long-term, complex tasks
—recurrent pressures to make binding decisions and be accountable for
  their consequences
—sense of finiteness and the reality of death and suffering
—desire to provide for a secure and livable future
—fear of loss, failure, and embarrassment
—concern for the practical implications of ideas and ideals.

Adults want the hard-won lessons of these concerns to be respected, especially when it comes to discussing complex social issues that already impact directly on their lives. Precisely because they are adults, they expect and deserve to be treated as peer teachers at the same time as they are students who come together to learn something new. Here is the painful part—the something new must be created, reinvented, artistically fashioned by the "old" people and implemented from within the context of their "old" lives. There is no fictional escape to a new planet or a new frontier or the innocent hopes of youth; wherever we go, our lives go with us.

In the United States economy, the "old" people are caught in pervasive cultural patterns that make deep learning difficult to practice. Meeting the person in a learning situation means simultaneously working with and challenging cultural assumptions. Here are some big ones.

Time—Too Little

How often have you heard people express worries that they do not, or will not, have enough time? Time is in surprisingly short supply in the United States. For teachers dealing with social change, this fundamental shortage leads to several impossibilities at once. There will never be enough time to master all the complexities of a really adult problem, yet the limited hours set aside for addressing the problem as a group seem already too much, given people's overcrowded schedules, multiple jobs, separated families. The upshot is that busy adults can so thoroughly devalue their real possibilities for reflection and action that they never come together in the first place. In effect, we leave ourselves alone and empty-handed in exactly the areas where, as practicing adults, we most need resources from one another.

Adult learners need to be reassured that it is possible to address a social change issue over time without being constantly swallowed up in its complexities. They need to be able to see a structure that ensures some protection for the rest of their commitments as they open themselves to discussion of demanding new issues. Prevailing social change rhetoric tends to idealize people who have made totalized, radical life changes. But the truth is that most people—the people we actually hope to live and learn and work with—do not choose that road. Everyday heroism is quieter, more contradicted and overlapped with everyday responsibilities. Deep learning as a social process needs to acknowledge these limited contributions and organize them into a more powerful whole. People will find ways to endure an intolerable frying pan when the only alternative they see is jumping into the fire.

Mobility — Too Much

The United States economy puts people constantly on the move. From "career movers" to migrating farm workers, we are forced to uproot our families with distressing frequency in order to avoid unemployment. Within this cultural pattern, the potential for continuity through ongoing church communities is a welcome respite and a major advantage for adult education programs. Adult learners need communities where they can trust enduring relationships to transcend momentary differences of opinion.

Mobility happens in the mind, as well. Television timetables have conditioned us to move quickly from one topic to another, assimilating information only in small, prepackaged chunks. Thinking skills — ability to sustain attention and work with others to analyze issues in depth — are often woefully out of shape. Deep learning gives these skills stretching and strengthening. People have to continue working with the learning group over a period of time, taking actions that address the recurrent roots of their problems. Otherwise, they will walk away only cynical and sad, wiser but depressed.

Living the Tension through Community

This combination of too little time and too much mobility makes for a constant level of stress and insecurity in daily life. Most adults worry; we are kept awake at night by the tension between what we envision or desire and what we perceive as possible. For teachers of adults, what is important to note is that people often experience these pressures alone. An adult-centered educational process must be compassionate, structured to teach people through their own participation how to build and find support in community. And there must be a reliable practice of forgiveness that people can fall back on when the going gets rougher because of resistance and repression. Social change is a long haul, and we need to take care of one another along the road.

That central value — community — directs that deep learning programs be as participatory as possible in their design. It is easy to fall into practices that contradict an expressed desire to build community. We know that many people in the learning group have insights to offer to the planning process, but we give them ready-made programs instead of trusting and challenging them with adult tasks that include decision making. We know that famous guest speakers will not always be available and may well be "burnt-out" by the time they are invited to speak, yet we set up programs that depend on outside experts. We know that we ourselves get tired, that we need to develop new leadership and share the load with more than the eight or ten stalwart souls who find themselves on every volunteer committee, but we rarely take time to invite, train, and support the new leaders. We know that there will most certainly be calls to respond to other complex social issues in the future, yet we set up short-term programs that expose people to narrow curriculum content without teaching them a process upon which we can all build next time around.

With deep learning, the teacher's time sense is based on a vision of community organizing and long-term leadership development. Rather than planning one big presentation that "covers" an issue, the teacher gives relatively more attention to an analysis of the people in the community and their existing social structures. The goal is to develop ongoing networks that will persevere and continue working with a persistent problem. This shifts the teaching task from one-time curriculum preparation to giving careful attention to follow-up phone calls, making connections, and arranging support for co-leaders.

Deep learning necessitates a truly adult way of interacting, based in the realization that we need one another if we are to have the difficult, groundbreaking discussions necessary to come up with new answers. Learning by dialogue offers the opportunity to practice and receive the compassion and forgiveness that should be the hallmark of community. This is plain hard work. It challenges teachers and students to articulate opinions with a critical eye to the experiences that have shaped them, to hear something new as they listen to one another's stories, and to reevaluate their current situations and choices in the light of shared values.

Teaching in Earthquake Country

Adult teaching at its best is nonviolent practice. The key is to meet the person first and the issue second. Nonviolence does not mean avoiding conflicts; it means meeting conflicts with the conviction that the opponent is a valued human being. An example is in order here.

Teachers who raise basic social issues are often targets for "magic bullet" questions aimed at interrupting uncomfortable discussions. During the peace movement of the early 1980s, "What about the Russians?" was the magic bullet aimed at killing criticism of United States military policy. In the Catholic parishes where I was working, this question was rarely a request for information; it was an invocation of totalized fears and the specter of a dehumanized enemy. I understood it to mean, "You are on my turf and it is time for you to leave." But I also understood the fears behind that question to be quietly shared by a good number of audience participants who would not put themselves out on a limb to raise such a public objection. The most fiery and passionate questioners were people in a position of particular vulnerability, and therefore perhaps unwittingly exposed to the possibility of learning and change. It would have been neither appropriate nor fruitful to address their questions as debating points.

As a teacher interested in deep learning, I did not assume that visible, meaningful change would happen right there and then. I wanted to give that questioner (and the rest of the audience who would have gotten quieter by then, listening for the fight) something new to think about on the way home. As an organizer, I knew that I needed to turn some of the questioner's evident energy toward helping my project instead of opposing it. Neither of us was going to magically disappear any time soon; we were connected, and we needed each other whole.

Proceeding from this stance — that I needed her — I learned to ask publicly for the deeper feeling behind her question, and especially to ask her to articulate what values she felt were being lost or violated. This usually elicited explanations beyond the stock question, explanations mixed with strong emotions and contradictory elements. I would then begin to sort out defiance from shared hopes, working to hold up every element with which I could honestly and solidly identify (platitudes and avoidances are deadly in this situation). Having recognized the person and what she cared about and was afraid of losing, I was in a position again to invite her to help me address the problem at hand.

This worked because we were dealing not just in terms of debate but in terms of praxis. First I would get closer to the person, then return with her to the task of getting closer to the problem. We usually had before us a tangible common representation of the issue — what Freire calls a *codification* — or an array of projects under consideration. In my role as teacher, this gave me a place to refocus energies and regather the group. Saul Alinsky used to say that every meeting should ask participants to make some decision together, otherwise it is wasted time from an organizing point of view. Deep learning proceeds by means of manipulable objects of discussion that call forth group decisions. Especially for adults, there is no knowing without doing. Adults make decisions, take on responsibilities, respond to problem situations. As we come to new understandings, we initiate transformation in our daily lives. As we experience the process and consequences of that transformation, we understand in yet a newer way. We begin to move ourselves and our worlds.

In a deep learning process, the inevitable and legitimate question will arise, "What can we do about this?" Each group will have to decide for itself which actions are appropriate and manageable. These decisions will surely vary from group to group; I have no preconceived universal right answers to offer here. Deep learning entails experimentation, sometimes calling us to say *no* to certain aspects of the dominant culture. What is essential is that adult participants decide together during their meetings to take some manageable, visible steps in response to the concerns they have shared. Those steps should be things that they themselves can control, that make sense in the light of their community history and style of working together, that are acts of public witness as well as personal survival.

Part of the decision-making task of the group is to schedule a time when they will gather to evaluate the effects of their experiments. Evaluation is an indispensable part of the adult learning process. What have we learned about taking a moral stand, about ourselves as People of God? What have we learned about the actual rootedness of this problem in people's lives? How are our next steps different because of what we have learned by these experiments? With whom will we take the next steps? The grey-haired ladies of one conservative San Francisco parish were shocked when their chosen project (to hand out peacemaker holy cards after the Masses one Sunday) was met with accusations that they were communists. Taking and evaluating that small, concrete step together opened the way toward deeper analysis and more effective planning for change in the parish.

Working together on a project makes it possible for diversity to be a contribution rather than an impediment to the group. The issue is not to homogenize one another according to some dominant image, but to discover what light can be shed by the different life perspectives of each participant. Adult learners have widely varying life experiences that predispose them to hear the message of a deep learning process in disparate ways. It may be that their experiences open them to new ideas, or it may be that profound feelings freeze them into preconceived and unassailable channels of thinking. For example, the majority of United States Catholic parishioners today have been formed as adults by World War II, McCarthyism, and the Cold War. Criticisms of the military-centered economy, however thoughtful and based in ethical principles, may ring anti-American to some. They may be threatened by talk of a truly global economy or a world that is not centered around current United States life-styles. The place to start with such people is by valuing and reevaluating their formative experiences, eliciting the contradictory hopes and disappointments inherent in them—not by trying to erase or escape their influence. People are attached to their lives, but their lives contain fault lines along which there can and will be movement.

Adult learners, like children, can be reliably expected to be at different points in their developmental processes as people of conscience. In 1982, the *Challenge of Peace* pastoral letter called United States Catholics to a new maturity as believers and as citizens. For some, it was confusing to read the distinctions the bishops made between binding moral principles and best prudential judgments. Many harbored the sneaking suspicion that if the bishops had really meant what they said, they would have said it in pre-Vatican II "lay down the law" terms. Deep learning practices a new and more nuanced language of moral consideration. This is obviously a lesson that will take time to learn. Conscience formation is an ongoing process of living out values in the context of everyday community, not in an isolated personal relationship with God or in one blinding flash of insight. Teachers need to know how to recognize and interrupt arguments that arise out of individual developmental differences, even as we encourage discussion of real disagreements about points of content.

Adult learners cannot be assumed to know automatically how to sustain a dialogue that admits divergent opinions on loaded social-change issues. Our tendency is often to polarize, to cast issues in terms of right and wrong and locate ourselves firmly among the saved. This is a purified and unreal projection; most people actually live somewhere in between on complex issues. We balance adult responsibilities with our visions of a just society and of ourselves as agents who do (or don't) have the power to shape our own lives. Teachers need to hold up a mirror in which people can recognize themselves as they really are, beyond the idealized masks that get dragged out for purposes of moral one-upmanship.

If teaching is a particularly valuable form of meeting, how does the teacher deal with avoidance? Surrounding any small group of activists, there is a large body of people who have *not* been working for changes and who are also needed to create a more livable world. What of the people who are well organized to maintain a destructive status quo? For a teacher who is committed to a group of people or to an issue, there has to be a way to impact on the people who hold the problem in place. Problem maintenance happens on many levels: there are policymakers (probably distant, insulated) and there are the people who live with an issue from day to day. Empowering the victims begins from the recognition that those who suffer the consequences of unjust policies can also have a hand in transforming *or* preserving them. It is simultaneously hopeful and problematic to realize that people are not merely suffering victims; *we* have a hand in maintaining our problems, as well. Teachers can expect increasing internal resistance as external opponents begin to be dealt with. Adult learners are attached to their lives, and their lives embody aspects of collaboration in their own limitations.

Freire calls this bind the *internalization of oppression.* Sometimes it makes the most accessible, close-to-home issues the most difficult to deal with. Home is the place where we are the most vulnerable, but it is also where we can be the most powerful. The world is interconnected enough that careful praxis, whether on local or larger issues, begins to work like an earthquake; movement on one front enhances movement on another. People cannot be expected to like earthquakes, especially when they are adults who have something to lose. When the world is literally shaken to its foundations (and past them, sometimes), we are compelled to reach beyond the comfort of the everyday. Previously settled issues come painfully into question once more. It is a precarious and also a very fruitful time. Nobody likes it, but it means that the world is still alive.

Teachers of deep learning do not cause earthquakes; that would be massive egotism to suppose. The earthquakes are ripe for happening within the contradictions of the living world. People's lives are not monolithic; they are overlapped with heavy moving plates and fault lines. As a teacher accompanies adults who are intent upon change, s/he recognizes and works with earthquakes, entering consciously into the moments that open up for deep learning. Teaching means gathering people to prepare for coming upheavals and to rethink and restructure their communities in the aftermath of each major shaker.

Living in earthquake country changes us as teachers, makes us grab onto those around us, sends us searching for a stable doorway in which to stand until the shaking stops. It also teaches us how precious are our lives together, the safety of our children, the lights in the night, and the clean water we share. Deep learning with people in the midst of earthquakes is therefore an abundant process, a way of meeting and being filled with life in all its contradictions. It gives us a way to rejoice in the hopes that we embody together.

16

The Prophetic Challenge in American Seminary Education

GEORGE WILLIAMS WEBBER

A Bit of Background

Union Theological Seminary in New York City was a major locus of Bob Brown's seminary involvement during a large part of his ministry. Following a compressed B.D. education from 1943-1945, he returned from 1948-1951 for his Ph.D. study and a year as a young instructor. He was back as a professor from 1953-1962. As a colleague during those years, I well remember his concern that the faculty examine fundamental questions about the task and direction for theological education in a rapidly changing society. Although the seminary president and many of the faculty dismissed such concerns as a "young man's interest," a number of us, including several older faculty members, were convinced that critical issues demanded attention. Perhaps Bob's decision to leave Union for Stanford in 1962 reflected something of our mutual feeling that not much was going to change. And his faculty colleagues for the most part found it incomprehensible that anyone would leave the greatest seminary in the world for a college teaching position.

When Bob was persuaded to return to Union in 1976, it was with the confidence that the seminary was now prepared to wrestle seriously with issues of its basic task, the appropriate style of its life as a faith community, and its role in the life of church and community as part of its mandate to train future clergy and scholars. His discovery that such issues were not on the seminary's agenda to any serious extent serves to underline my thesis that theological education has not given attention to the urgent questions of vocation, style and direction. In spite of the serious studies, often critical, that have appeared in recent years, I suspect that the life of most of our seminaries, whether the denominational schools or the university-related non-denominational seminaries like Yale and Harvard, are not all that different from the time Bob Brown entered Union almost 40 years ago. In the face of that reality, this brief essay seeks to examine the persistent issues that must be addressed and then provide some clues as to possible directions for a seminary that accepts its prophetic mandate in the life of the faith community.

Persistent Issues

The tension between the seminary as a graduate school of religion and a professional school for preparing clergy for ministry has often posed a serious dilemma or outright contradiction rather than offering challenge for a creative interaction. In a medical school, the faculty for the most part continue to practice medicine, while the bulk of seminary teachers are scholars. Far too often those who teach in the "practical" disciplines feel like second-class citizens. Note that this issue is raised as a sober concern that will always demand attention, as a tension that needs to be maintained as a creative reality and challenge to appropriate balance.

This leads directly to a second issue, namely the long struggle to change field work, a source of income for the student and occasionally a valuable part of preparation for ministry, into genuine field education. Large foundation grants and much effort have been devoted to this task. But the struggle goes on, with field education still a modest element in the time and energy of most seminary students. They know that the academic requirements are what seem to matter. And effective field education requires financial investment to insure excellent placements in locations that cannot afford field-work stipends.

A third persistent issue, although not seen as such by the vast majority of seminaries, is the limited scope of those to whom their resources are available. In a city like New York, where 80 percent of the Protestants are in Black congregations, 10 percent in Hispanic, and only 10 percent in traditional White churches, the great majority of clergy have had little access to college education and virtually none to graduate theological schools. But they are pastors of vital, Spirit-filled congregations whose presence in the cities of our land can be a powerful witness to the Gospel and whose potential to challenge the oppression of our day is unlimited. And what a culturally deprived education for the traditional seminary constituency to be educated in isolation and often ignorance of this large and vital segment of the Christian community! In a multicultural world, experience in a multicultural context would seem to be urgent.

A final issue, among many more that might be discussed, arises in the present uncertainty in the churches regarding for whom the seminaries are training leadership about critical elements of mission and ministry. What for today's churches is the role and mandate for the ordained clergy persons? Given the emphasis over the past 30 years on the critical ministry of the laity, what are the implications for the work of the clergy? How does their ministry empower rather than hinder the emergence of strong lay ministry? Such questions do not adequately intrude themselves into the seminary curriculum. A corollary to this concern relates to the nature and mission of the congregation in contemporary society. If, in the familiar phrase, "The church exists for mission as a fire exists for burning," then there must be critical issues in the training of clergy for a mission-oriented church, for a community of Christians intent on continuing the ministries of Jesus in their community. The traditional model of preacher, teacher, counselor, and administrator will need modification, to say the least. What will be required for the clergy person to equip laity to confront the oppressive forces in our society, challenge the values of a consumer-driven economic order, face hostility and conflict, and in all this discover the joy in such faithfulness?

This is not an exhaustive list, but it illustrates the issues that cry out for attention in the world of theological education.

A Smattering of Helpful Biblical Insights

In reflecting on these issues, a cluster of biblical passages provides helpful insight and challenge for the task ahead. These are offered as illustrative of the vital role that such interaction with scripture can play in defining our task in theological education.

Luke 5:37

The need always to seek new wineskins for the forms of the life of the Christian community is a reminder that we must always be open to the new patterns that our ministry requires. But how hard it is for either a seminary or a congregation to examine its present life and practice with this question: What is the purpose, in a world that is changing dramatically? This "new wineskin" emphasis is a reminder of the basic Protestant principle that we must always seek new patterns in order to witness to the Gospel in a changing world. So it must be for the faithful seminary.

Philippians 2:5-11

This passage suggests the urgency of living out the incarnation in the life of a Christian community. One implication for a seminary would be the importance of taking seriously its own context, being a relevant presence in the place where God has located it. When Bob Brown was called back to Union in the 1970s, he spent a semester talking with Christians throughout Latin America, sharing his concern that the seminary relate to the needs of churches under oppressive forces. Again and again, he found people intrigued that a seminary was expressing such a concern, many of which would then ask, "And what is Union doing about its own neighborhood? How does it relate to Harlem and the city?" This was a challenge that urban seminaries have not often been willing to face, but seems implied by the Philippians passage.

Jeremiah 29:4-7

This passage, indicating that the task of the faith community is to seek the shalom of the place where it finds itself has *become the mandate* of the New York Theological Seminary. What a challenge to convince the clergy and laity of the churches all through the city that God put them there to work for shalom, to be a sign of God's presence and to seek justice, to demonstrate peace. A seminary, as an expression of a faith community, would seem also called to demonstrate the same commitments.

Ephesians 4:11-16

Here is a powerful definition of the purpose of a faith community as a base within which the members are to engage in the task of growing toward maturity, to the stature of full personhood as modeled in the life of Jesus. The clues found in these verses suggest (1) that all members are called to ministry, (2) that a faith community fulfills its mandate to empower the growth of all its members when it encourages them to speak the truth in love and (3) that it recognizes the mutual interdependence of all who are part of its life.

The implications of these clues will be more apparent as we explore a cluster of suggestions for seminaries that are determined to accept the challenge of prophetic life and work.

Modest Suggestions for Seminaries Seeking To Be Faithful to Their Prophetic Calling

The "Lifestyle" of a Seminary

There is no avoiding the reality that the quality and patterns of life in the seminary make a profound, if often unconscious, impact on the students. This is not to argue that the seminary community is a "church," a definition that is often rejected, but to affirm the fact that every seminary, Roman Catholic, Protestant, or Orthodox, is a Christian community of persons with commitments, whose relationships, priorities, personal lifestyles and choices reflect and express the reality of their faith. Integrity would seem to demand that the seminary demonstrate in its own life the faith which it professes. In the faculty where I teach, we sometimes ask, with genuine seriousness, are we demonstrating some of the elements of the alternative community that we discuss in our classes; are we in fact reflecting the reality of a community where the impact of the "Jesus Way" is being made specific and visible?

Of course our lifestyles take many forms, but surely the Christian community must demonstrate alternatives to our consumer-driven society and reject the explicit values of American life. Might not faithfulness today require us to live as exiles in our own land? For faculty, this suggests concerns about personal values and lifestyle. What does it mean to heed the familiar slogan, "Live simply that others may simply live?" What are the implications for how we teach? One faculty reported that they have decided to stop teaching disciplines and start teaching students. In one instance, where the struggle to learn Greek was a major hurdle for the average student, a gifted New Testament professor undertook to understand the experience and context of her students, and then demonstrated that they had an unrecognized ability to master the material and meet the challenge that led to a sense of accomplishment.

Another element in the lifestyle of a seminary might be to demonstrate the importance of evaluation and feedback in the effort to be faithful in ministry. At New York Theological Seminary, several times each year an outside consultant with no axe to grind or long-term involvement in our work would be asked to examine over the course of 3 to 4 days some element of our program of operation. He would read what we said we intended—for example in the D-Min program—talk to present students and graduates, visit classes, and then report to us what was in fact happening. Such feedback would inform our practice and often lead to significant changes. This emerges out of our own need to be clear about what we are doing, but it also models a way by which a congregation should also ask regularly about its own life and ministry, facing the risk of discovering areas of self-deception, programs that do not accomplish what they are intended to do, wineskins that have grown old and no longer are useful in ministry.

The bottom line is simply this: the need for the seminary community to demonstrate models of integrity that relate to the life and work of faith communities for which the students are being prepared.

The Constituents of the Seminary

Clues come immediately to mind. The first is the importance for seminary students to come with significant life experiences that can form the basis for their theological study and reflection. Biblical faith is always the task of making sense out of one's life experience and determining what God is calling one to be and to do. Without much experience outside of the arenas of family, church and school, the student is not adequately prepared to make good use of seminary study. One dean noted that he would like to admit students only when they had spent at least several years immersed in experiences beyond the college years. Of course, these days in many seminaries half or more of the students come as "second career" persons. Sadly enough, many of these older students seem interested only in preparing for very traditional ministries and do not necessarily come with maturity and strong potential for pastoral leadership.

Another way of pointing to the same concern is to urge all students to engage in significant (i.e., over a period of time) multicultural experiences.

Two-week trips designed to provide new global perspectives simply do not often provide a sufficiently vital experience. Surely the clergy of our time desperately need to be at home outside the homogeneous culture that characterizes so many of our traditional congregations.

Equally important is the challenge to the seminaries to provide educational opportunities for the large number of potential and present leaders in vital faith communities who have not had access to graduate education. We live in an urban world where the vitality of Christian witness is powerfully expressed in Black, Hispanic, Korean, and independent churches. The presence of their leaders in seminary life, because they find education there creative and helpful in their own work, brings vitality and integrity to the life of the whole community.

Another clue in relation to the student constituency comes from a pattern of education that was given focus years ago by the faculty of Union Seminary in Richmond. The curriculum was devised to insure that in each course three elements were always present and given serious attention: the knowledge that the professor sought to impart, the areas where growth in personal maturity was encouraged, and the competencies in the practice of ministry that were to be developed. With such emphases, the professor is clearly not teaching a discipline, but teaching students, concerned about the whole person's preparation for faithful life and ministry.

From the witness of the Spirit in Latin America, from women's studies, and from the Black church in this country have come a strong hint that in seeking knowledge of the faith, the student must discover the process of relating action and reflection, faith and obedience, theology and life. This is sometimes referred to as "praxis," and suggests that biblical faith is always dialogous between the context in which the believer is located and the stories of faith. Knowledge learned in isolation from concrete situations is likely to be an opinion, not a vital faith understanding.

A concern for the growing maturity of a student has never come easily to seminaries where scholars focus on getting material across. And the result of sixteen years of previous "schooling" is evident in my struggle to get students to believe me when I urge them, upon reading a book, to tell me what difference it will make in their faith and life, what implications for their ministry, and what made it worth reading for them. They seem convinced that they must prove to me they read the material and can demonstrate where they take issue with the author, but no more. I have taken to requiring a regular "journal" where reflections upon one's growth as a person is the focus.

The element of competence in the practice of ministry is not easy to encourage in a classroom. This suggests that we simply must work at bringing about an authentic dialogue in the classroom with effective field education. The key word is integration, and this will force seminaries in their curriculum to discover patterns of collegial teaching and a new attention to the role of "practical theology." But it also suggests that perhaps the seminaries should pay attention to a project of some years ago of the United Methodist Church, the Young Pastor's Program, which assumed that much that was needed in the actual practice of ministry could best be developed in the early years in parish life. Newly assigned clergy were expected to spend regular weekly time in peer learning, with experienced mentors, where they worked on their preaching, examined their pastoral practice, sought to develop teaching skills and administrative competence. In this context they learned the importance of feedback, of regularly examining one's practice, and developing clear priorities and goals whose achievement had to be checked out. It required each person to gain clarity about his or her own gifts of ministry, to work at enhancing their usefulness, and to determine a definition of the pastoral work in which he or she was engaged. In our rapidly changing society, the need for continual reexamination must become second nature.

The Role of the Seminary in the Life of the Church

Biblical people are called to be a bi-focal community, demonstrating in their life together an alternative expression of human unity and at the same time called to fulfill in society their mandate to seek shalom, to point to, work for, demonstrate signs of righteousness and justice in the midst of the oppression and divisions that deny God's reign. Heresy is not false faith, but holding firm to community as central and ignoring the call to continue the work of Jesus in the context where God has placed his people. For in seeking shalom, we discover our own shalom, as Jeremiah reminded the exiles in Babylon. A seminary also ignores its context and the responsibility it bears to seek shalom at its own peril of lapsing into heresy. New York Theological Seminary determined that one element of its vocation was to seek every possible means to convince the churches of the inner city, large and small, to recognize that God placed them there not to provide a community for survival alone, but as a base from which to engage in the struggle against oppressive structures and to work for shalom. The faculty of the seminary were also called to enter personally into the struggle in New York City by using their gifts in congregations, community organizations and other groups working for peace and justice.

Another dimension of the prophetic task is suggested by a recent discussion of the role in the life of El Salvador of the six murdered Jesuit professors. Here I paraphrase remarks made by Hugh Lacey, Swarthmore College, at a consultation in Philadelphia, using them to suggest how a seminary faculty might function.

The seminary faculty discover that they must link their commitment to the pursuit of truth with a strong link to liberation and justice in United States society. They do not just talk, but attempt to shape their teaching and research activities so that they address issues of injustice and division. They send students to interact with poor communities; they document the conditions of growing homelessness, racism, and violence; and they put the weight of the seminary's authority on the side of those who are suffering. In doing this, they pose a challenge to the denominations and congregations that show no interest in such concerns. In brief, they seek to develop a seminary in which the quest for knowledge goes hand in hand with shaping social institutions in which there is the widest possible inclusiveness, a diversity of perspectives, visions and people. Only in such efforts may we hope to prepare students for careers that will enable their congregations to join in the struggle for social transformation, to seek shalom for all God's children.

A Final Word

Our seminaries, with their tradition of academic freedom, their opportunity to test new ideas and new patterns for ministry, and their continuing dialogue with congregations, have a unique and urgent opportunity to unmask the deceptions of congregations, model new wineskins for faithful ministry, prepare prophetic and creative leaders for the future, and in their own life model a community that stands as a sign of God's activity in the world.

17

Religion and the Secular Media

LEON HOWELL

Very few people reading this book are likely to disagree with the following proposition: We get far too little coverage of religion in our secular media, and what we do get is largely incomplete, irrelevant or inadequate.

This is true although several polls demonstrate a high level of religious involvement among the American people and a desire to read, see and hear more about the religious dimensions of our common life. An extensive investigation of religious coverage in newspapers released in October 1989, by Religious News Service (RNS) also demonstrated that readers rated the quality of religion coverage lowest among nine "special interests," such as sports and education.

Television and radio today have almost no interpretive coverage of religion and report only its most superficial aspects, mostly about personalities or scandals. Newspapers—the focus of this discussion—do little better. Articles come out of nowhere, point nowhere. "The amount of space given religious news is minuscule and inconsistent," David Anderson said at a 1991 media and values conference held by *Christianity and Crisis* magazine, "compared, say, to the news one receives—day after day—about the sprained ankle of a football running back."

One of the best daily newspapers, the *Washington Post*, rarely writes about religion as a vital part of life; it usually buries a Saturday religion page somewhere behind the real estate section. The articles that do appear with the church advertisements are an indigestible lump. Religion coverage is justified only because papers "get a lot of church ads, and they have to put something around them," said the legendary Ben Bradlee, managing editor of the *Washington Post* during its Watergate glory, in a notorious 1983 quote.

The problem is likely to get worse. In spite of increasing recognition by some newspapers that religion deserves serious treatment, what the industry calls the "news hole" grows smaller as papers add more graphs (*USA*

Today influence), make their stories shorter (television's influence), and print more fluff. That leaves even less space for serious religion news and reflective reporting.

The quality of reporting also seems to be in decline, in spite of some examples of a more complete concept of coverage. One of the rare national radio or television journalists who devoted attention to religious issues, Mike Maus, left CBS Radio in 1991 to go with public radio in Minnesota because CBS did not value his expertise sufficiently to offer a competitive contract. With the all-but-total demise of United Press International in 1992, David Anderson—who for more than 20 years covered religion for UPI—is no longer available to hundreds of large and small papers (he is now the Washington correspondent for RNS). And John Dart, whose work for the *Los Angeles Times* helped give it a reputation for as good a coverage of religion as any newspaper, was transferred in late 1991 to the San Bernardino bureau, one of several reporters over 50 years old who have been moved to suburban news coverage. Dart, then president of the 150-member Religion News Writers of America (the guild for religion reporters for secular papers), warned in early 1992 that during times of economic pressure, "stereotypical stories about religion look increasingly attractive to inattentive editors."

The reasons all this is true are complex. Religion is not an easy beat to cover. Local churches as well as denominational structures often want coverage only on their terms. It takes sophistication, which some have, to endorse the positives and the negatives of media examination. As well, religion brings a dimension of the transcendent into a medium that wants to emphasize facts and figures.

And without question some aspects of religion make readers as well as reporters uncomfortable: the end-of-the-world prophets, for example. And how other than as spectacle to write about the 1990 baptism of Earnest Byner of the Washington Redskins in the jacuzzi of all-pro defensive back Darrell Green, with some 20 or more born-again members of the Redskins saying that Byner's all-pro performances in 1991 and 1992 stemmed from that experience? The Redskins are careful not to claim that they won football's 1992 Super Bowl because of their strong religious inclinations, but Green did call a crucial replay reversal of a touchdown by the Philadelphia Eagles in 1990 "a big, big gashing blow to the face of the devil."

For decades religion coverage tended to be compartmentalized, placed on the religion page, relating with no interpretive function church events and institutional pronouncements. Both because they are leery of the complex emotions surrounding religious expression and because in some cases they do not take seriously the religious forces that motivate much human activity, newspapers have shied away from serious religious coverage.

But this limits drastically our understanding of the role religion plays in everyday life. A good example: In 1985 a black Pentecostal minister who had been very active in civic affairs was killed in a car wreck in Portland,

Oregon. The whole community turned out for his funeral. In her report on the funeral, the religion writer at the *Oregonian* told, in the minister's words, how his political and civic involvement grew out of his faith. The story as written was not published; it was edited to list what groups the minister had supported and who attended the funeral.

If some reporters are advocates for coverage of religion in their papers, they often are not respected by their peers. Helen Parmley, long-time religion writer, told the RNS interviewers that when she worked at the *Dallas Times-Herald* it "couldn't decide whether religion was a good beat or a punishment tour. One morning the city editor got mad at the police reporters and said, 'alright, you write religion today.' "

The result is that too few papers have reporters with the interest or skills to cover religion, in part because some of the most able see it as a dead-end job.

So one gets writing like this from an August 1992 Knight-Rider story which took off from the good idea of reexamining religion as practiced on campus: "Some Jewish students are uncomfortable on a campus tainted with anti-semitism."

Or take a small but illuminating story from 1987 of reporting so poor it would not be tolerated in most sections of a paper. As William Sloane Coffin was preparing to leave New York's Riverside Church after a remarkable ten years, one critical source always appeared in stories about his Riverside tenure. I saw it in AP, *Washington Post*, and CBS news stories. The Men's Class, with a 145-year history and a high period when John D. Rockefeller, Jr., taught it (then at another location), said such things as Coffin's having brought "infamy, disrepute and near destruction" to Riverside. But when I visited the Men's Class I found that only two women — who by its charter could not officially be members — were in attendance at its weekly meeting. Confused, I asked at the information desk if I had gone to the right place. "That's it," I was told. "It's usually two or three women and two men. Sometimes it's as many as six." The angriest man, over 80 years old, was not a member of the church, I later learned. But established media accepted "The Men's Class" as critics of Coffin in a church of more than 2,500 members without asking any questions.

Little wonder then that few religion writers can unpack complex issues such as the 1991 Orthodox churches' threat to leave the National Council of Churches (NCC) because it was "too liberal." (An excursion, to use a Bob Brown technique: The NCC has become a decidedly different organization from its heyday in the 1960s and is a story worth telling with care. But one writer says all attacks on the NCC play well with editors. So the *New York Times* in 1983 had three articles within the year quoting the Institute on Religion and Democracy as attacking the NCC's "leftist bias" without bothering to discover that IRD, a tiny organization with a political perspective, got 91 percent of its funding from foundations with a right-wing political agenda.) How organizations with as different a cultural as well as theological history as the mainline Protestant, African-American denominations and Orthodox work together is a complex and interesting story. But the reporting on the NCC-Orthodox debate did not tell how important this arena had been for warring Orthodox branches, or how public roles for women in worship (much less ordaining them) was a primary Orthodox criticism.

Even full-time religion reporters at *Time* made a mishmash of a cover story on why attendance in mainline churches has declined (May 23, 1988). *Time* contrasted the decline in mainline membership with growth in Catholic, Southern Baptist and evangelical churches, without any examination of the civil war within Southern Baptists, the loss of priests and changing nature of American Catholicism, and the growing pluralism and polarity in evangelical congregations. The point is that this article did nothing to help readers grasp the complex church situation across the board in the United States.

One final comment about why coverage of religion is hard in secular newspapers. David Anderson points out that many journalists and editors care a great deal about personal ethical questions — not letting a source pay for lunch, not being flown to visit a nuclear reactor by an interested party — and the ethical problems of others, such as Jim Bakker's financial maneuverings or Gary Hart's affairs. "But rarely does this behavioral concern translate itself into any question of values."

A lot more could be written about the problems. But what has already been presented leaves the question of whether poor coverage of religion is important and what can be done about it.

The short answer: It is important that so essential a matter as the impact of religious belief on our values and actions is not reported by the mass media in a serious way. Yes, alternate sources of information exist for persistent people. But imagine what it would mean if people of sensitivity and skill were sought to report on religion for the mass media and were supported by their editors.

There is some reason to hope. Over the past two decades or so, religion as news — from the civil rights movement to Islamic fundamentalism to television preacher scandals — has gained more status in some newspapers. So the *New York Times* hired Peter Steinfels, editor of the serious Catholic lay journal *Commonweal*, to write about religion, and the *Wall Street Journal* added Gustav Niebuhr (grandson of H. Richard and great-nephew of Reinhold). In 1991 Peggy Fletcher Stack was hired by the *Salt Lake City Tribune* to undertake serious religion coverage, not least of the Mormon church; three-quarters of Utah's population are Mormons. Religion is one of the subjects for Barbara Reynolds, a recent graduate of Howard Divinity School and columnist for *USA Today*. And, of course, Bill Moyers is the very model for a person who displays personalities in all their permutations, including religion.

Such trends should be encouraged. A public demand for more and better coverage — not just of church activities but of the deep portents of religious signs and symbols; not just on a religion page but R.O.P. (run of paper) — could bring results.

One organization I know well, Bread for the World (Barbara Howell is a long-time staff member), has developed useful ways of calling attention to its issues: local Bread for the World members write letters to the editor, make phone calls, develop contacts with editors and editorial writers, send materials. Specific issues, legislative efforts, and concerns are emphasized, but the religious undergirding for their efforts is not hidden. I once saw a Bread for the World file of more than 110 positive editorial responses to increased funding for WIC (the feeding program for women, infants, and small children at nutritional risk), in large part stimulated by Bread for the World efforts.

It helps if editors know that people care about the quantity and quality of coverage of issues about religion. The RNS study cited earlier showed that a desire for religion coverage was in a strong middle position among nine "special interest" topics such as business and sports. But the sample rated the quality of religion coverage last among the nine issues.

The possibilities are there. They need to be fanned. Who knows? Religious people may even encourage their papers to spend more time seeing the world from below — from the point of view of the poor, the persecuted, the suffering that Robert McAfee Brown has so emphasized in his life's work.

For too long the religious dimensions of American life have been under-reported. We have reason to raise our voices to address this issue.

18

Is There a Prophetic Future
for the Church?

CARTER HEYWARD

What does it mean for liberal Christians to say publicly today, "I am Christian"? For many of us, this question sparks a sense of crisis that is only secondarily a crisis in language. It is primarily a crisis in our common life, the sort that moved Bonhoeffer from his prison cell to call for a "religionless Christianity" and, a generation later, prompted Dorothee Soelle to write "An Essay in Theology After the 'Death of God'."[1] With Dietrich and Dorothee, and with Bob and Sydney Brown, we see that we are a people and a planet in deep trouble.

But hasn't it always been so? Is there anything really new about where we are today, we Christians and Jews in the United States and elsewhere in the so-called First World, home to about one-third of the earth's population? Have times really changed all that much from what they were when Bonhoeffer urged Christians to lay aside our priestliness and live for others, a vocation he himself followed to the Gestapo gallows?

Surely the claims of good and evil upon us are no greater or smaller than ever. Now as before we have choices to make, those of us with the economic, sexual, racial, ethnic, religious, or other structures of social privilege that generate options from among which we can choose where to put our bodies, with whom to stand, how far to go, and at what risk. In that sense, little has changed. As Elie Wiesel notes, these questions of good and evil "are troubling, and they are eternal."

But something is, I believe, changing today among many liberal Christians. Our moral vision is being sharpened. Through the collapse of much of totalitarian communism and the subsequent economic, military, and moral advance of monopoly capitalism globally, we see more clearly that either we as nations, religions, and other cultural communities will learn to live with others or we will die, all of us. We are waking up to the fact that we are in crisis; that it is *ours* as a global matrix; and that it is a matter of our living or dying *together*. Bill Coffin eloquently describes our common task: "The big news of the twentieth century is that henceforth it is the world as a whole that has to be managed, and not just its parts." Citing Michelangelo's admonition, Coffin warns us that "hell is truth seen too late" and urges us to be the prophetic church while there is still time.

In recent decades, reacting against the hollowness of liberal politics and religion in the United States, numbers of justice-seeking people from various faith-traditions have used the term *liberal* in largely disparaging ways. *Liberals* have been for us people and policies shaped by class-cultivated aversion to conflict, hence to dwelling upon serious differences among us. By contrast, *liberation* theology (oxymoron in the mainline churches) and *liberation* politics (oxymoron in the United States government) have signaled a stronger commitment to a justice that can be forged only in struggle. With Robert McAfee Brown much in mind, I want us to reclaim liberalism — specifically, those of us who are Christian — to take back liberal Christianity and insist that the liberal church be the liberation church. I want the term *liberation church* to begin to sound redundant to those of us who are in it and to others as well.

For too long, white liberal Christians have spoken superficially, if sincerely, of unity, harmony, reconciliation, and peace when there has been no real peace and can be none as long as the foundations of oppression are left intact within and beyond the churches. Allan Boesak speaks powerfully to this danger which has held South Africa in its grip since 1990, when the white minority government began slowly to dismantle apartheid. Boesak and others are warning the liberal readership of this book (most of us) against the tendency of those with social power (including us) to *misappropriate* the values, cultures, and languages of others in order to secure their (often, *our*) own privilege. Thomas Peterson demonstrates how, in fact, white, eurocentric United States culture has done just that in relation to Native American peoples and traditions. Through Richard Cartwright Austin's reflections on our lack of an adequate environmental ethic, we are reminded of the extent to which our relationship as humans with the earth has also been one of gross misappropriation rather than "mutual sustenance." And both Denise and John Carmody represent the male-female relationship, cross culturally and historically, as having been secured by men's violent misuse of women's lives and bodies and, still today, by most men's failure to acknowledge this or change it. Speaking directly to this failure on men's part, John Carmody writes, "If male Christian leaders want to demonstrate their courageous embrace of the dangerous memory of Jesus, they ought to make the amelioration of the plight of poor women and children their first order of social business." *Misappropriation*: to benefit from women's living and loving and working; to learn from women's values, feelings, cultures, and creativity; and to love and honor women without a fundamental transformation of the sexist and heterosexist underpinnings of patriarchal society and religion.

Let's look a little more closely at these dynamics of misappropriation. Gregory Baum points out that the Quebec Roman Catholic bishops' statement on the economy (May 1, 1992) "can be read in a reformist and in a more radical way." What Baum doesn't go on to say needs nonetheless to be said—that, in any context, reformism always runs the risk of misappropriating resources such as labor, ideas, dreams, and money from those with the least social power. This is because, while the reformist agenda intends to benefit marginalized people, the benefits bestowed cannot alter existing power arrangements. In a capitalist economy, this means that the goals, strategies, dreams, and language of the poor must be manipulated by those with economic power in such a way as to bring about just enough reform to meet the poor's demands for change, yet never enough to deprive the powerful of their privilege. This is misappropriation—when those with wealth and status adopt languages of "justice," "struggle," and "love of neighbor" without relinquishing their power.

One of the most pressing, double-edged dangers those of us who are liberal Christians in the United States face is that we increasingly will misappropriate the resources of others (for instance, ripping off the faith tradition and stories of Jews for our own Christian purposes) *and* of having our lives, stories, labor, and languages taken over by those with greater social power. I think of Bush going on about peace, jobs, and the stability of the family, and of Quayle holding forth on economic justice, and of John Paul II advocating the dignity and well-being of women, and of all those white Christian men exploiting the work and love and dreams and bodies of women for our own good.

Misappropriation aims to render invisible our particularities as human and other creatures, how we are different, and therefore where we may conflict. It is the smoothing over of rough painful places without bothering to find out how the wounds were inflicted and whether they may be deep, infected, even deadly. It is a way of doing business as usual in the language of the oppressed. It is the way we Anglos and other Europeans historically have dealt with Native peoples in the Americas and with African-Americans, Asian-Americans and, here in the North, with Latino/as. Misappropriation is the primary means by which liberal white Christians have engaged the religious and cultural traditions of others whom we have considered our friends. This volume in honor of Robert McAfee Brown should be read as a challenge to liberal Christians to stop stealing from our friends; a challenge to churchmen to stop ripping off churchwomen; and a call to us all to stop standing by quietly as our commitments, theologies, and moral languages are distorted by those in high places who gladly will speak of "justice" and "peace" as long as their power is held secure and unchanged.

If there is a prophetic future for the church, and there must be if the church of the twenty-first century is to be anything other than a rubber stamp for the unfettered advancement of global capitalist institutions, values, and privileges, we Christians must learn our way beyond misappropriation, on both sides of this disingenuous politic. Otherwise, our Christian and Jewish and Islamic and other religious languages of love, justice, and liberation will have become a primary language of late monopoly capitalism. And we will find ourselves, much as Hereticus warns, hailing the "prophet-motive" as the sacred basis of our lives and of our nation as the United States of Jesus Christ.

Such *christofascism* (originally Dorothee Soelle's word) is not farfetched at all. We need to be aware that an immense amount of activity, time, money, and determination is being organized in the United States today by coalitions of right-wing Christians, right-wing Republicans, white racists, and proudly sexist/heterosexist groups. Here in this nation, as in Germany, much of Latin America, and elsewhere in the world, those who have created God and His [sic] will in their own image are on the move and should be taken seriously.

Globally, many of these fascists are Christians, and nearly all of them (be they Christians, Jews, Muslims, others) adhere to rigid patriarchal principles and, hence, are bound together by one primary religious principle: *misogyny*, the hatred of women, and the requisite control of women's bodies and lives (which is why *heterosexism* is a staple of sexist patriarchy). The joining of women-hating with capitalism's profit-driven obsession constitutes a daily, and long-term, danger to all women and children in the world, especially those who are poor (most women and children in the world) and those who, on the basis of whatever social privilege we may have had, have become feminists: that is, women who have chosen to defy patriarchal practices and challenge patriarchal institutions rather than simply joining them as good daughters of the fathers.

If there is a prophetic future for the church, it will be in an immensely costly solidarity with women and children, especially poor women and children, women and children of color, and feminist, womanist, and lesbian women — inside the church as well as elsewhere in the world. The church, if it is to be prophetic, must therefore be not only a liberation movement but moreover a *feminist liberation* movement. Even this volume fails, on the whole, to raise up this challenge forcefully.

What then is the prophetic work of a church that is a feminist liberation movement? a church that does not misappropriate the lives, labor, and love of the very people it is most committed to standing with? (If the reader has become suddenly anxious about the emphasis on feminism in this essay, perhaps he or she can read this anxiety as a barometer of patriarchal socialization. For the attitude that "women's issues" ought not be overstated or centralized is at the very core of the liberal church's failure to comprehend or respond adequately to issues that have been raised for over two decades by women of all colors and more recently by gay men and lesbians).

We feminists and others in liberal churches and religious traditions who wish to be involved in justice-making today need, as these essays suggest, to re-vision the work of liberation, to re-image it as a deeper and broader historical project than many of us have until recently. First, as Richard Cartwright Austin writes, it is not just *human* well-being that is making demands on us but moreover the liberation of other creature-species and the earth itself. We need a *deep-ecology* if we, as a whole people and planet, are to survive. Second, we need also to learn our way beyond violence as our primary means of social control and of resolving conflict. This is the vision in Pia Moriarty's piece on education. We need to help one another, collectively and individually, learn *nonviolence* as the only way of life to which we, as Christians, can aspire in good faith. This is not to say that we white Christians in the North have any right whatsoever to tell Nicaraguan peasants, South African laborers, or people of color here in United States cities that they should not arm themselves in the struggle for justice. We white people have a lot more to learn than to teach about nonviolence. But we can learn with one another, across color lines where this is possible, what it really requires for us to strive together toward nonviolence as a way of shaping community and society and as a daily practice and spiritual discipline. Karen Lebacqz's suggestion that empathic suffering, along with participation in the struggle for justice, may provide a bridge between us and our enemies reflects an image of nonviolence as a basic way of life. It seems to me that these moral requirements—that liberation be our aim for the earth and all creatures, not just humans, and that our goals and means, wherever possible, be nonviolent—are what can, and will, distinguish the prophetic church from nonprophetic, or false-prophetic, churches that are no less passionate in their vision.

If there is a prophetic future for the church, it will be in our learning genuinely how to love our neighbors—that is, how to wish them no harm; how to wish them peace, even if they may wish us dead, and, at the same time, how to make no peace with their oppression and their violence. If we are learning this, we are likely to be expanding the genuinely moral horizon of the earlier reformers about whom Richard Shaull speaks. John Coleman is right: such a church necessarily will disrupt the status quo. If we are not annoying those who hold social, economic, and ecclesial power in place, we are not a prophetic church and we will not be.

Elie Wiesel urges us to remember—like Lot's wife—to look back, lest we turn not to salt but to ice. Janet Walton reminds us that prophetic liturgy invites us to remember and, in this way, to move forward: "[enacting] the impossible in all manner of ways: to hear it, to demand it, to live into it."

What is this "impossible," this "ideal," to which a prophetic religious community is called? Is it not the way of nonviolence? Is it not deep ecology? Is it not feminist liberation movement? Is it not a refusal to misappropriate the labor and resources of others? Is it not what Mary Judith Dunbar, Jerry Irish, and George Webber envision as the basis of excellent education—ways of learning and teaching that draw us into the work of justice? ways of learning that take as their starting point the needs of the poor?

Leon Howell thoughtfully explores why religion isn't a more popular media item today. The media, like mainline religion, is a creation of patriarchal capitalism. Like the church, the mainstream media looks to "the fathers" for instruction, definition, and permission. Why then should the media be any more interested in religion than religion is in the media, as long as *both* are playing the roles of obedient children in the patriarchal household? Both media and church today function largely as "opiates of the people." As long as this is so, and to the extent that it is, neither church nor media can be prophetic. Neither makes news, and both strike most thoughtful people either as outrageously irresponsible or as boring.

If we are to be a prophetic church, we probably will not be big news makers. Prophets are seldom stars. But we will not be boring. Rather, in Pia Moriarty's words, we will be "dangerous people," like Bob Brown.

Notes

1. *Christ the Representative* (Philadelphia: Fortress, 1967). Translated by David Lewis from the German *Stellvertretung—Ein Kapitel Theologie nach dem 'Tode Gottes'* (Kreuz Verlag, 1965).

A Selected Bibliography of the Works of Robert McAfee Brown

LINDA W. GLENN

The career of Robert McAfee Brown has spanned both sacred and secular worlds, encompassing the arenas of ecumenism, antiwar activism, struggles for justice and human rights and liberation theology. His many readers have been fortunate that Brown has been a prolific writer of his experiences and perceptions of those significant times in which he participated and that he continues that production into retirement.

A complete bibliography of the writings of Brown would be more than a chapter—it would be a hefty work by itself. At this point, articles for magazines and journals number at least 360, with probably 50 more to be discovered and cataloged. Twenty-five books of his own and dozens of prefaces, forewords and conclusions in other works testify to his extraordinary output. A list of periodicals publishing his writings runs the gamut from *A.D.* to *Workers with Youth.* His work reflecting the diversity of his career, Brown has analyzed theological and social issues and thus built bridges of communication to groups outside university and seminary walls. Participating in times of social transformation and interpreting those times has given Robert McAfee Brown a distinctive role among Protestant religious leaders.

This bibliography is, of necessity, abbreviated. Brown's books are presented chronologically with annotation, followed by his edited and translated works. One area of tremendous output has been his chapters in edited collections, which are listed. Articles by Brown which explore his own professional development as well as writings about him are also included in this bibliography. The myriad articles, prefaces, conclusions, sermons, foreign language editions, reviews of his books, book reviews by him—all wait to be assembled, even as other works flow from his typewriter/computer as swiftly and penetratingly as they have throughout the past forty years.

Books by Robert McAfee Brown

P.T. Forsyth: Prophet for Today. Philadelphia: The Westminster Press, 1952.

Brown's doctoral dissertation, *P. T. Forsyth, The Man and His Work,* was later published as *P. T. Forsyth: Prophet for Today.* Presenting an introduction to his writings and theology, often in Forsyth's own words, Brown comes to the conclusion that Forsyth (1848-1921) was a member of no "school" even after his revolt as a theological "liberal of liberals."

The Bible Speaks to You. Philadelphia: The Westminster Press, 1955 and *The Bible Speaks to You.* Second Edition, Philadelphia: The Westminster Press, 1985.

Beginning as curricular material for the Presbyterian Church, this book has become a classic of biblical interpretation for youth, adult laypersons and clergy. Attentive to substance, but presented in an unconventional style for the fifties, *The Bible Speaks to You* was reprinted nine times in thirty years. In the new preface for the 1985 edition, Brown expresses chagrin at the sexist language contained in the earlier edition, but reluctantly decides to "Let the text stand . . . for what it is—a product of the early 1950s with whatever strength and weaknesses such a product embodies."

The Significance of the Church. Philadelphia: The Westminster Press, 1956.

The Significance of the Church was one of a series of twelve volumes, the highly successful Laymen's Theological Library (of which Brown was the general editor), appearing in the late 1950s when many people were returning to churches. Often used in small groups, the purpose of the series was "to remind the layman that he is a theologian." In *The Significance of the Church,* Brown historically and doctrinally explores the Protestant heritage, emphasizing the meaning of the Reformation and the need for continual reformation within the church.

An American Dialogue: A Protestant Looks at Catholicism and a Catholic Looks at Protestantism, co-authored with Gustave Weigel, S.J. Garden City, New York: Doubleday and Co., 1960.

In *An American Dialogue* Brown traces the Protestant tradition as well as the history of Catholic-Protestant relations, exploring problem areas of understanding, suggesting ground rules for rewarding dialogue with Roman Catholics. Both Brown and Fr. Weigel begin with the assumption that America is no longer a Protestant nation but a pluralistic one, a view also held by Will Herberg, who wrote the foreword. Although there is no rebuttal to each section, this book was one of the first genuine interfaith conversations.

The Spirit of Protestantism. New York: Oxford University Press, 1966.

The Spirit of Protestantism is a comprehensive survey of Protestantism—history, affirmations, concerns—its essence, which Brown calls its "spirit." Seeing Protestantism as more than a negative Catholicism or a halfway faith between Catholicism and agnosticism, he explores issues that contribute to the chasm between Protestants and Catholics. He places a preface at the end of the work because, for Protestants, the Christian life is "the story of a pilgrimage." Extensive notes and bibliography are included.

An Observer in Rome. Garden City, New York: Doubleday and Co., 1964.

From September 29-December 4, 1963, Robert McAfee Brown attended the Second Session of the Vatican Council as one of the few invited Protestant observers. *An Observer in Rome* is a firsthand glimpse of the workings of the Council—a lively, humorous and thoughtful recounting of the daily proceedings, conflicts and finally, accomplishments. He describes himself as moving from "bouyant optimism" to "chastened optimism" in this book of theological and personal reflections.

The Collected Writings of St. Hereticus. Philadelphia: The Westminster Press, 1964 and *The Hereticus Papers*, Vol. II. Philadelphia: The Westminster Press, 1979.

St. Hereticus, everyone's favorite observer of the theological and ecclesiastical scene, presents two collections of his columns. His trenchant observations date from 1955, and he is "closely identified" with Robert McAfee Brown.

The Presbyterians. Glen Rock, New Jersey: Paulist Press, 1966.

This short tract (29 pages) is part of the Paulist Press Ecumenical Series. It explains the basic beliefs and structure of Presbyterianism, including several pages devoted to issues which separate Presbyterians and Catholics. It also contains the answer to why Presbyterians preach longer than anyone else. Answer: "They don't. It only seems longer."

The Ecumenical Revolution. Garden City, New York: Doubleday and Co., 1967.

Brown's experiences, anticipations and concerns for ecumenical progress were chronicled in his first major work after Vatican II, *The Ecumenical Revolution* (partially based on the William Belden Noble Lectures at Harvard). A survey of ecumenical development—"from diatribe to dialogue"—revealed the rapidly changing ecumenical climate in the 1950s and 1960s. He also examined Jewish-Christian conversation and secular ecumenism, the action of the church to the world. An Ecumenical Bibliography and "Milestones on the Road to Christian Unity Chart" are included.

Vietnam: Crisis of Conscience, with Abraham J. Heschel and Michael Novak. New York: Association Press, Behrman House, and Herder and Herder, 1967.

This inexpensive ($.95) volume, co-authored by a Protestant, a Catholic, and a Jew, was jointly printed by publishing houses of the three major faiths with all royalties going to Clergy and Laymen Concerned About Vietnam. Addressed to the troubled consciences of Christians and Jews, the book was a handbook to be used in congregations and religious groups to clarify the issues surrounding our involvement in Vietnam and to guide groups into effective action.

The Pseudonyms of God. Philadelphia: The Westminster Press, 1972.

The Pseudonyms of God spans fifteen years (1955-1970) of Brown's theological journey, including articles, essays, and speeches— how Brown's positions have been reshaped by events, how he sees God working in the world in unlikely arenas. His own dissent is recorded in the section encompassing civil rights and anti-war speeches. "The Supreme Pseudonym" interprets ways in which Christ is found in the world—and if not found, "it will not be because he is not there, but simply because we have been looking for him in wrong places."

Religion and Violence. Second Edition. Philadelphia: The Westminster Press, 1987. Originally published as *Religion and Violence: A Primer for White Americans.* Stanford: Stanford Alumni Association, 1973.

Brown relates his personal journey from pacifism, to support of World War II, to nonviolence, to the recognition of the limits of nonviolence. He reaches his conclusions based on the inadequacy of nonviolence to deal with issues of social justice. Focusing on the roots of violence, the structures of violence in society and the voices of the third world, he sees the task of our churches as "to embody revolutionary nonviolent love." The Kaethe Kollwitz charcoal drawings add a powerful and anguished dimension which portray the consequences of violence. Brown includes an annotated reader's guide and an introduction to the second edition, commenting on more contemporary issues of religion and violence in the late 1980s.

Frontiers for the Church Today. New York: Oxford University Press, 1973.

Originally prepared as lectures, *Frontiers for the Church Today* provides both a critique of the ills of the church and ideas for its reform. Using the metaphor of church as frontier, Brown explores the challenges in recent ecumenical, technological and cultural developments, concluding with images of the church as servant, counterculture and pilgrim.

Is Faith Obsolete? Philadelphia: The Westminster Press, 1974.

In *Is Faith Obsolete?* Brown extends an invitation to consider the reality of faith to those outside the Christian tradition, and, as usual, interprets issues of faith to lay people. Exploring various approaches to faith, he uses the writings of Elie Wiesel, who has struggled with the devastation of the Holocaust to an eventual faith stance. Within the context of liberation theology, Brown challenges white, middle-class congregations to recognize their part in the economic inequalities of the third world. Much of this book was presented as the Frank H. Caldwell Lectures at Louisville Presbyterian Theological Seminary.

Theology in a New Key. Philadelphia: The Westminster Press, 1978.

Theology in a New Key was one of the first introductions to liberation theology. Using musical metaphors (established harmonies, diminished sevenths), Brown explains recent liberation themes in Catholic and Protestant churches, analyzes liberation theology and responds to criticism—the "chords of discord." He challenges North Americans to rediscover the Christian message in light of liberation themes. Both Spanish and English resources and an annotated bibliography are included.

Creative Dislocation—The Movement of Grace. Nashville: Abingdon Press, 1980.

Using creative dislocation as an image for pilgrimage, Brown writes on the personal changes and professional crises in his own faith journey during the 1960s and 1970s. He reflects upon his "dis-locating" from Stanford to Union Theological Seminary to Pacific School of Religion; his involvements in the arena of political issues—civil rights, Vietnam, South Africa, Latin America; and his personal insights into marriage, friendship and aging.

Making Peace in the Global Village. Philadelphia: The Westminster Press, 1981.

Brown defines global peacemakers as a remnant of the faithful within the church, along with those outside who side with the oppressed. In *Making Peace in the Global Village* he presents a positive process for peace which involves middle-class congregations looking at their social structures and working to transform them. Questions for study groups interested in peacemaking are included.

Elie Wiesel: Messenger to All Humanity. Notre Dame, Ind.: University of Notre Dame, 1983.

In *Elie Wiesel: Messenger to All Humanity* (published by a Catholic university press), Brown introduces readers to the writings of a Jewish storyteller and Holocaust survivor. Wiesel's works are explored and liberally quoted. Brown also urges Christians to examine their own theological and ethical responses to the Holocaust, insisting that the Holocaust is a problem for both Christians and Jews and one about which both faiths must struggle.

Unexpected News — Reading the Bible with Third World Eyes. Philadelphia: The Westminster Press, 1984.

Aiming at a wide audience, Brown presents ten familiar Bible stories to be seen through the "optic of the poor," the eyes of the powerless. These well-known biblical figures are presented in a new framework, putting the reader in the shoes of those in the third world. In an epilogue Brown confesses that his own life-style reflects his North American theological interpretation and that it is not third world Christians "who are giving us a hard time; rather, the *Bible* is giving us a hard time."

Saying Yes and Saying No: On Rendering to God and Caesar. Philadelphia: The Westminster Press, 1986.

What happens when issues of justice and peace conflict with the policies of the United States government? In *Saying Yes and Saying No,* Brown examines some of those concerns — national security, foreign policy (U.S., South Africa, and Poland), nuclear armaments, sanctuary and our own response of saying yes or saying no. Brown's own "Barmen Confession" of theological issues begins this book; a letter to his grandson concerning world peace marks the conclusion. Reflection questions at the end of each chapter make this a valuable resource for discussion groups in congregations.

Spirituality and Liberation: Overcoming the Great Fallacy. Philadelphia: The Westminster Press, 1988.

To overcome the fallacy that our lives are divided into "spiritual" and "material," Brown writes of spirituality and liberation as two ways of talking about the same thing. Attempting to provide a vision of wholeness, he uses a variety of images, traditions and figures — those who "[show] by deeds what cannot be shown by words."

Gustavo Gutiérrez. Atlanta: John Knox Press, 1980 and *Gustavo Gutiérrez: An Introduction to Liberation Theology.* Maryknoll, N.Y.: Orbis Books, 1990.

A friend of liberation theologian Gustavo Gutiérrez, Brown has written two books about him, both biographical and theological. The first was part of the series, "Makers of Contemporary Theology." The latter *Gustavo Gutiérrez* is a new work incorporating a small amount of material from the first. Brown uses Gutiérrez's writings and conversations in explaining liberation theology and exploring the differences between Latin American and North American theology. An extensive bibliography of Gutiérrez's writings, representative writings of Latin American and North American theologians, and Brown's annotated notes on Gutiérrez follow.

Persuade Us to Rejoice: The Liberating Power of Fiction. Louisville: Westminster/John Knox Press, 1992.

Brown's recent work looks at fiction and its power. Examining issues such as waiting, questioning, grace, brokenness and pain, he explores, among others, stories of Silone, Wiesel, Camus, Buechner and Walker.

Liberation Theology: An Introductory Guide. Louisville: Westminster/ John Knox Press, 1993.

Originally lectures given at the Chautauqua Institute in New York in 1991, this small book explains the new ways of viewing the world, people, God, and the church that liberation theology offers, as well as the innovations it offers for the faith of North Americans.

Books Edited by Robert McAfee Brown

The Challenge to Reunion. Edited with David H. Scott. New York: McGraw-Hill, 1965.
A Cry for Justice: The Churches and Synagogues Speak. Edited with Sydney Thomson Brown. Mahwah, N.J.: Paulist Press, 1989.
The Essential Reinhold Niebuhr: Selected Essays and Addresses. New Haven, Conn.: Yale University Press, 1986.
Kairos: Three Prophetic Challenges to the Church. Grand Rapids, Mich.: William B. Eerdmans Publishing Co., 1990.

Books Translated by Robert McAfee Brown

Casalis, Georges. *Portrait of Karl Barth.* Garden City, N.Y.: Doubleday and Co., 1963.
de Dietrich, Suzanne. *God's Unfolding Purpose.* Philadelphia: The Westminster Press, 1957.
Dumas, Andre. *Dietrich Bonhoeffer: Theologian of Reality.* New York: Macmillan Company, 1971.

Works by Robert McAfee Brown in Edited Collections

Humor
"The Gospel According to St. Hereticus—Scripture Lesson for Easter." In *Witness to a Generation: Significant Writings from Christianity and Crisis, (1941-1966),* edited by Wayne H. Cowan, pp. 160-162. Indianapolis: Bobbs-Merrill Co., 1966.
"Introduction—Baked Corn Pone: Theology Off Key." In *Mark Twain Himself: Humor, War and Fundamentalism,* edited by William McLinn, pp. xxv-xxvi. Dubuque, Iowa: Kendall/Hunt Publishing Co., 1983.
"Making the Bible Relevant." In *Bittersweet Grace: A Treasury of Twentieth-Century Religious Satire,* edited by Walter D. Wagoner, pp. 170-172. Cleveland: World Publishing Co., 1967.

"Oral Roberts and the 900-Foot Jesus." In *And the Laugh Shall Be First: A Treasury of Religious Humor,* compiled by William H. Willimon, pp. 148-156. Nashville: Abingdon Press, 1986.

Interfaith Dialogue and Vatican II

"American Catholicism Now: A Protestant View." In *Where We Are: American Catholics in the 1980s,* edited by Michael Glazier, pp. 11-25. Wilmington, Del.: Michael Glazier, 1985.

"An American Protestant View." In *Looking Toward the Council: An Inquiry Among Christians,* edited by Joseph E. Cunneen, pp. 110-116. New York: Herder and Herder, 1962.

"The Church's Ecumenical Outreach." In *American Catholic Exodus,* edited by John O'Connor, pp. 66-85. Washington, D.C.: Corpus Books, 1968.

"The Coming of the Messiah: From Divergence to Convergence?" In *Human Responses to the Holocaust: Perpetrators and Victims, Bystanders and Resistance,* edited by Michael D. Ryan, pp. 205-223. New York: The Edwin Mellen Press, 1979.

"Commentary: *Gaudium et Spes.*" In *Documents of Vatican II,* edited by Walter M. Abbott, S.J., pp. 309-316. New York: Herder and Herder, 1966.

"The Ecumenical Movement." In *Encyclopedia of Religion,* edited by Mircea Eliade, Vol. 5, pp. 17-27. New York: Macmillan and Co., 1986.

"An Ecumenical Pioneer." In *One of a Kind: Essays in Tribute to Gustave Weigel,* edited by John Courtney Murray, S.J., pp. 87-95. Wilkes-Barre, Penna.: Dimension Books, 1967.

"The Ecumenical Venture." In *Theologians at Work,* edited by Patrick Granfield, pp. 1-21. New York: Macmillan Co., 1967.

"Giving Account of Hope: A Brief Report on the U.S." In *Sharing in One Hope: Commission on Faith and Order,* pp. 113-127. Bangalore Conference, Geneva, Switzerland: World Council of Churches, 1978.

"Gregory Baum: Personal Encounters." In *Faith that Transforms: Essays in Honor of Gregory Baum,* edited by Mary Jo Leddy, N.D.S., and Mary Ann Hinsdale, I.H.M., pp. 3-7. New York: Paulist Press, 1987.

"The Holocaust as a Problem in Moral Choice." In *Dimensions of the Holocaust,* pp. 47-63. Evanston, Ill.: Northwestern University, 1977.

"The Holocaust as a Problem in Moral Choice." In *When God and Man Failed: Non-Jewish Views of the Holocaust,* edited by Harry James Cargas, pp. 81-102. New York: Macmillan Co., 1981.

"*Humanae Vitae*: A Protestant Reaction." In *Contraception: Authority and Dissent,* edited by Charles E. Curran, pp. 193-215. New York: Herder and Herder, 1969.

"Introduction." In *The Jews: A Christian View,* edited by F. W. Foerster, pp. vii-xxvii. New York: Farrar, Strauss and Cadahy, 1961.

"Introduction." In *The Open Circle: The Meaning of Christian Brotherhood,* edited by Joseph Ratzinger, pp. 9-18. New York: Sheed and Ward, 1966.

"Introduction." In *A Pope for all Christians? An Inquiry into the Role of Peter in the Modern Church*, edited by Peter J. McCord, pp. 1-12. New York: Paulist Press, 1976.

"The Issues Which Divide Us," in *American Catholics: A Protestant-Jewish View*, edited by Philip Scharper, pp. 59-124. New York: Sheed and Ward, 1959.

"Memory Redeemed?" in *Memory Offended: The Auschwitz Convent Controversy*, edited by Carol Rittner, R.S.M., and John K. Roth, pp. 191-201. New York: Praeger, 1991.

"Nine Steps to Unity." In *Living Room Dialogues*, edited by William Greenspun, C.S.P., and William Norgreen, pp. 31-42. Glen Rock, N.J.: Paulist Press, 1965.

"Nine Steps to Unity." In *Steps in Christian Unity*, edited by John A. O'Brien, pp. 61-73. Garden City, N.Y.: Doubleday and Co., 1964.

"Paul's Contribution to Ecumenism." In *Paul VI: Critical Approaches*, edited by James F. Andrews, pp. 94-112. New York: Bruce Publishing, 1970.

"The Protestant Tradition of Religious Liberty." In *Religious Liberty in the Crossfire of Creeds*, edited by Franklin H. Littell, pp. 20-24. Philadelphia: Ecumenical Press, 1978.

"Secular Ecumenism: The Direction of the Future." In *The Religious Situation*, edited by Donald R. Cutler, pp. 395-422. Boston: Beacon Press, 1969.

"Some Are Guilty, All Are Responsible." In *Abraham Joshua Heschel*, edited by John C. Merkle, pp. 123-141. New York: Macmillan Co., 1985.

"The Spirit and Forms of Protestantism." In *First Steps in Christian Renewal*, edited by Abigail McCarthy, pp. 81-109. Wilkes-Barre, Penna.: Dimension Books, 1967.

"Starting Over: New Beginning Points for Theology." In *Religion in America*, edited by George C. Bedell, Leo Sandon, Jr., and Charles T. Wellborn, pp. 523-526. New York: Macmillan Co., 1982.

"They Could Do No Other." In *The Courage to Care: Rescuers of Jews During the Holocaust*, edited by Carol Rittner, R.S.M., and Sandra Myers, pp. 143-147. New York: New York University Press, 1986.

"Twilight: Madness, Caprice, Friendship and God." In *Between Memory and Hope*, edited by Carol Rittner, R.S.M., pp. 177-187. New York: New York University Press, 1990.

"Unity—Dream or Demand." In *Sermons to Men of Other Faiths and Traditions*, edited by Gerald Anderson, pp. 129-139. Nashville: Abingdon Press, 1966.

"What Is Ecumenism and Why?" In *Ecumenism: The Spirit and the Worship*, edited by Leonard Swidler, pp. 15-37. Duquesne, Penna.: Duquesne University Press, 1967.

Justice and Human Rights

"Further Reflections on Freedom Riding." In *The American People in the*

Age of Kennedy, edited by David Kennedy, pp. 155-156. West Haven, Conn.: Pendulum Press, 1973.

"The God Who Stamps Out War." In *Preaching on Peace,* edited by Ronald J. Sider and Darrel J. Brubaker, pp. 45-51. Philadelphia: Fortress Press, 1982.

"Introduction." In *Economics for Prophets,* by William Owensby, pp. vii-ix. Grand Rapids, Mich.: William B. Eerdmans Publishing Co., 1988. Sidney Thomson Brown co-authored the introduction.

"Introduction." In *Mark Twain Himself: Humor, War and Fundamentalism,* edited by William McLinn, pp. xxv-xxvi. Dubuque, Iowa: Kendall/Hunt Publishing Co., 1983.

"Martin Luther King, Jr." In *Beyond Vietnam: A Prophecy for the 80s,* pp. 17-20. New York: Clergy and Laity Concerned, 1982.

"The Need for a Moral Minority." In *Speak Out: Against the New Right,* edited by Herbert Vetter, pp. 118-126. Boston: Beacon Press, 1982.

"No Promise Without Agony: An Address to Educators." In *Agony and Promise: Current Issues in Higher Education,* pp. 265-267. San Francisco: Jossey-Bass, Inc., 1969.

"Poverty and Conscience." In *Poverty and Social Justice: Critical Perspectives,* edited by Francisco Jimenez, pp. 127-138. Tempe, Ariz.: Bilingual Press, 1987.

"The Religious Right and Political/Economic Conservatism." In *Border Regions of Faith: An Anthology of Religion and Social Change,* edited by Kenneth Aman, pp. 258-263. Maryknoll, N.Y.: Orbis Books, 1987.

"Theological Implications of the Arms Race." In *Peace in Search of Makers,* edited by Jane Rockman, pp. 92-102. Valley Forge, Penna.: Judson Press, 1979.

Liberation Theology

"After Ten Years—Introduction." In *The Power of the Poor in History,* by Gustavo Gutiérrez, pp. vi-xvi. Maryknoll, N.Y.: Orbis Books, 1983.

"Biblical Concepts of Idolatry." In *Sanctuary: A Resource Guide for Understanding and Participating in the Central American Refugee's Struggle,* edited by Gary MacEoin, pp. 55-61. San Francisco: Harper and Row, 1985.

"Christians in the West Must Confront the Middle East." In *Beyond Occupation,* edited by Rosemary Radford Ruether and Marc Ellis, pp. 138-154. Boston: Beacon Press, 1990.

"Freedom and Political Responsibility." In *Proclaiming the Acceptable Year,* edited by Justin L. Gonzales, pp. 116-123. Valley Forge, Penna.: Judson Press, 1982.

"Introduction." In *Anecdotes and Analysis from Nicaragua: Rice, Beans and Hope,* edited by Thomas Montgomery-Fate, Rafael Aragon, and José Maria Vigil, pp. ix-xi. New York: CIRCUS Publications, Inc., 1988.

"Learning from James Cone." In *A Black Theology of Liberation: Critical*

Reflections, by James Cone, pp. 164-169. Maryknoll, N.Y.: Orbis Books, 1986.

"Liberation Theology: Paralyzing Threat or Creative Challenge?" In *Mission Trends 4, Liberation Theologies in North America and Europe*, edited by Gerald Anderson and Thomas Stransky, pp. 3-24. New York: Paulist Press, 1979.

"1984: Orwell and Barmen." In *The Peacemaking Struggle: Militarism and Resistance*, edited by Ronald H. Stone and Dana W. Wilbanks, pp. 137-145. Lanham, Md.: University Press of America, 1985.

"A North American View." In *Evangelization and Politics*, edited by Sergio Arce and Oden Marichal, pp. 136-148. New York: CIRCUS Publications, 1982. Brown also wrote a "Special Introduction to the English Edition," pp. 7-15.

"A Preface and a Conclusion." In *Theology in the Americas*, edited by Sergio Torres and John Eagleson, pp. iv-xxviii. Maryknoll, N.Y.: Orbis Books, 1983.

"The 'Preferential Option for the Poor' and the Renewal of Faith." In *Churches in Struggle: Liberation Theologies and Social Change in America*, edited by William K. Tabb, pp. 7-17. New York: Monthly Preview Press, 1986.

"A Protestant Look at an Aggressive Papacy." In *The Church in Anguish*, edited by Hans Küng, pp. 177-185. New York: Harper and Row, 1987.

"Reflections of A North American: The Future of Liberation Theology." In *The Future of Liberation Theology: Essays in Honor of Gustavo Gutiérrez*, edited by Marc Ellis and Otto Maduro, pp. 491-501. Maryknoll, N.Y.: Orbis Books, 1989. This essay is also found in a paperback with the same material, *Expanding the View*, pp. 194-206, 1990.

"Response." In *Questions of Faith: Contemporary Thinkers Respond*, edited by Dolly K. Patterson, pp. 48-49, 76, 79. Philadelphia: Trinity Press International, 1990.

"The Significance of Puebla for the Protestant Churches in North America." In *Puebla and Beyond*, edited by John Eagleson and Philip Scharper, translated by John Drury, pp. 330-346. Maryknoll, N.Y.: Orbis Books, 1979.

"What Can North Americans Learn from Minjung Theology?" In *Commentary on Korean Minjung Theology*, edited by Jung Young Lee, pp. 35-47. Mystic, Conn.: Twenty-Third Publications, 1988.

"What Is Contextual Theology?" In *Changing Contexts of Our Faith*, edited by Letty Russell, pp. 80-95. Philadelphia: Fortress Press, 1985.

"What Kind of Messiah?" In *Social Themes of the Christian Year*, edited by Dieter T. Hessel, pp. 80-85. Philadelphia: Geneva Press, 1983.

Theology: Brown's Earlier Writings

"Classical Protestantism." In *Patterns of Faith in America Today*, edited by F. Ernest Johnson, pp. 9-51. New York: Harper and Bros., 1957.

"God's Pseudonyms." In *The Presence and Absence of God,* edited by Christopher Mooney, S.J., pp. 109-128. New York: Fordham University Press, 1969.

"Ignazio Silone and the Pseudonyms of God." In *The Shapeless God: Essays of Modern Fiction,* edited by Harry J. Mooney, Jr., and Thomas Staley, pp. 19-40. Pittsburgh, Penna.: University of Pittsburgh Press, 1966.

"Immortality," and "Soul (Body)." In *A Handbook of Christian Theology,* edited by Marvin Halverson and Arthur A. Cohen, pp. 183-185 and 354-356. Cleveland, Ohio: The World Publishing Co., 1969.

"Introductory Essay." In *How to Serve God in a Marxist Land,* Karl Barth, pp. 11-44. New York: Association Press, 1959.

"Military Chaplaincy as Ministry." In *Military Chaplains: From Religious Military to Military Religion,* edited by Harvey Cox, pp. 139-147. New York: American Report Press, 1971.

"New Directions in the Church Today." In *Great Religions of the World,* pp. 392-409. Washington, D. C.: The National Geographic Society, 1971.

"Order and Ministry in the Reformed Tradition." In *Reconsiderations: Roman Catholic/Presbyterian and Reformed Theological Conversation,* pp. 107-138. New York: World Horizons, 1967.

"P. T. Forsyth." In *A Handbook of Christian Theologians,* edited by Martin E. Marty and Dean G. Peerman, pp. 144-164. Cleveland, Ohio: The World Publishing Co., 1965.

"The Pseudonyms of God." In *Philosophy of Religion,* edited by Norbert O. Schedler, pp. 105-120. New York: Macmillan and Co., 1974.

"The Reformed Tradition and Higher Education." In *Christian Perspectives on Learning,* pp. 220-238. Grand Rapids, Mich.: Calvin College, 1979.

"Reinhold Niebuhr: A Study in Humanity and Humility." In *The Legacy of Reinhold Niebuhr,* edited by Nathan Scott, Jr., pp. 1-7. Chicago: The University of Chicago Press, 1974.

"Scripture and Tradition in the Theology of Karl Barth." In *Scripture and Ecumenism: Protestant, Catholic, Orthodox, and Jewish,* edited by Leonard J. Swidler, pp. 23-42. Pittsburgh, Penna.: Duquesne University Press, 1965.

"The Seminary in a Time of Revolution." In *Essay in Ministry,* pp. 42-49. Princeton, N.J.: Foundation for Theological Education, [no date].

"Story and Theology." In *Philosophy of Religion and Theology,* compiled by James McClendon, Jr., pp. 55-72. American Academy of Religion Proceedings, 1974.

"Sunday; June Fifth, Morning Service." In *(Doran's) Minister's Manual,* edited by Charles L. Wallis, pp. 158-159. New York: Harper and Row, 1972.

"A Theological Approach to the Inner-City Parish." In *Readings on the Urban Church,* edited by Robert Lee, pp. 349-356. Philadelphia: The Westminster Press, 1962.

"Theology and Education." In *The Scope of Theology,* edited by Daniel T

Jenkins, pp. 225-252. Cleveland, Ohio: The World Publishing Co., 1965.

"Theology and the Gospel: Reflections on Theological Method." In *Theology and Church in Times of Change,* edited by Edward Leroy Long, Jr., and Robert T. Handy, pp. 15-33. Philadelphia: The Westminster Press, 1962.

"What Does the Slogan Mean?" In *The Meaning of the Death of God: Protestant, Jewish and Catholic Scholars Explore Atheistic Theology,* edited by Bernard Murchland, pp. 170-184. New York: Vintage Books, 1967.

Vietnam

"The Berrigans: Sign or Model?" In *The Berrigans,* edited by William Van Etten Casey, S.J., and Philip Nobile, pp. 60-70. New York: Avon Books, 1971.

"In Conscience, I Must Break the Law." In *Starting Over: A College Reader,* edited by Frederick Crews and Orville Schell, pp. 188-193. New York: Random House, 1970.

"Introduction." In *Conspiracy: The Implications of the Harrisburg Trial for the Democratic Tradition,* edited by John Raines, pp. 1-35. New York: Harper and Row, 1974.

"Perspective for Readers." In *In the Name of America,* Clergy and Laity Concerned About Vietnam, pp. 1-14. Annandale, Va.: Triumph Press, 1968.

"A Protestant Reaction." In *American Catholics and Vietnam,* edited by Thomas E. Quigley, pp. 191-197. Grand Rapids, Mich.: William B. Eerdmans Publishing Co., 1968.

"Vietnam: Crisis of Conscience." In *New Theology No. 6,* edited by Martin E. Marty and Dean G. Peerman, pp. 229-242. New York: Macmillan Co., 1969.

Biographic and Professional Development

Articles by Robert McAfee Brown

"ABC: Assy, Bonhoeffer, Carswell." *The Christian Century* 88 (March 24, 1971): 369-371.

"Bennisons on Bennett." *The Christian Century* 87 (May 27, 1970): 663-664.

"A Campaign on Many Fronts." *The Christian Century* 82 (May 5, 1965): 577-579.

"Confession of a Political Neophyte." *Christianity and Crisis* 13 (January 19, 1953): 186-191.

"Discoveries and Dangers." *The Christian Century* 87 (January 14, 1970): 40-45.

"The Experiences of the '60s: A Few Lessons." *The Christian Century* 96 (January 3-10, 1979): 6-7.

"Former Ministers Speak for Themselves." In *250 Years at First Church in Amherst,* pp. 269-272. Amherst, Mass.: Amherst United Church of Christ, 1990.

"Making Friends with Time." *A.D.* (September, 1980): 16-18.
"The Meaning of Life." *Life* (December 1988): 83.
"My Most Memorable Christmas." In *My Most Memorable Christmas,* edited by Gerald Walker, pp. 87-89. New York: Pocket Books, 1963.
"The Not So Dow Scot." *Presbyterian Life* 7 (May 15, 1954): 15-36.
"Of Horsehair, Catgut and Sublimity." *The Christian Century* 96 (September 26, 1979): 911-912.
"On Earthquakes and Aftershocks." *The Christian Century* 106 (November 15, 1989): 1039-1040.
"Paul Tillich." *The Commonweal* 81 (January 21, 1966): 471-473.
"The Spirit's Eighth Gift." *Christianity and Crisis* 40 (February 4, 1980): 8-10.
"Starting Over: New Beginning Points for Theology." *The Christian Century* 97 (May 14, 1980): 545-549.
"Teaching Theology in a University Setting." *Union Seminary Quarterly Review* 22 (May 1967): 357-365.
"The Venerable Bushel." *The New Yorker* 30 (December 4, 1954): 52-53.
"Two Worlds: Beauty and Oppression." *The Christian Century* 97 (April 2, 1980): 378-380.
"We Have Met the Enemy." *The New Yorker* 29 (July 11, 1953): 58-61.
"What Is Shaping My Theology." *The Commonweal* 108 (January 30, 1981): 43-44.

Articles about Robert McAfee Brown

"Catholics' Protestant." *Newsweek* (January 14, 1963): 71.
Carmody, John T. "The Development of Robert McAfee Brown's Ecumenical Thought." *Religion in Life* 43 (Autumn 1974): 283-293.
Degman, James. "Robert McAfee Brown." *The Sign* (August 1967): 5-9.
Gonzalez, Justin L., editor. "Back to the Drawing Boards: Robert McAfee Brown." In *Proclaiming the Acceptable Year,* pp. 113-115. Valley Forge, Penna.: Judson Press, 1982.
Handy, Robert T. *A History of Union Theological Seminary in New York,* pp. 233, 318-322. New York: Columbia University Press, 1986.
Herhold, Robert M. "Bob Brown: Reluctant Radical." *The Christian Century* 88 (June 16, 1971): 745-747.
Lebacqz, Karen. "A Professor Named Brown . . . " *Pacific School of Religion Bulletin* 58 (Summer 1985).
Leona, Marian, S.N.J.M. "The Making of an Ecumenist." *Today* (October 1967): 4-7.
Nessan, Craig L. "Robert McAfee Brown: Herald and Apologist for Liberation Theology." In *The North American Theological Response to Latin American Liberation Theology,* pp. 171-185. Atlanta, Ga.: Scholar's Press, 1989.
"Pathfinding Protestants." *Time* (May 25, 1962): 84.
"A Protestant Columnist." *The Commonweal* 78 (January 4, 1963): 377-378.

Richardson, Lincoln. "Keeping Faith on Campus." *Presbyterian Life* 24 (September 15, 1971): 5-11.

Stahel, Thomas H. "Four Stories of Theology." *America* 136 (March 19, 1977): 230-233.

Thompson, Dean K. "Robert McAfee Brown Remembers Henry Pitney Van Dusen." *Journal of Presbyterian History* 56 (Spring 1979): 62-78.

"U.S. Protestantism: Time for a Second Reformation." *Newsweek* (January 3, 1966): 33-37.

Dissertation

Glenn, Linda W. *The Theologian as Social Activist: A Study of the Public Career of Robert McAfee Brown.* The Iliff School of Theology and the University of Denver, 1988.

Contributors

Richard Cartwright Austin serves on the faculty of the Appalachian Ministries Educational Resource Center.

Gregory Baum is Professor of Theology at McGill University in Montreal.

Allan Boesak directs the Foundation for Peace and Justice in South Africa.

Peter Brown is a professional photographer based in Houston, Texas.

Robert McAfee Brown is Professor Emeritus of Theology and Ethics at Pacific School of Religion, Berkeley.

Denise Lardner Carmody is University Professor and Chair of Religion at the University of Tulsa.

John Tully Carmody is Senior Research Fellow in Religion at the University of Tulsa.

William Sloane Coffin is Pastor Emeritus of Riverside Memorial Church, New York City.

John Coleman is Professor of Theology at the Jesuit School of Theology, Berkeley.

Mary Judith Dunbar is Professor of English at Santa Clara University.

Linda Glenn teaches American Religion at the University of Denver.

Carter Heyward is Professor of Theology at Episcopal Divinity School, Cambridge, Massachusetts.

Leon Howell is editor of *Christianity and Crisis.*

Jerry Irish is Provost at Pomona College, Claremont, California.

Karen Lebacqz is Professor of Christian Ethics at Pacific School of Religion, Berkeley.

Pia Moriarty teaches in the Program in Culture, Ideas, and Values at Stanford University.

Thomas V. Peterson is Professor of Religious Studies at Alfred University, Alfred, New York.

Richard Shaull is Henry Winters Luce Professor of Ecumenics, Emeritus, at Princeton Theology Seminary.

Dorothee Soelle lives in Hamburg, Germany, and teaches regularly at Union Theological Seminary, New York City.

Janet R. Walton is Professor of Liturgy at Union Theological Seminary, New York City.

George Williams Webber is Professor of Urban Ministry at New York Theological Seminary.

Elie Wiesel is author and Andrew Mellon Professor of Humanities at Boston University.

170

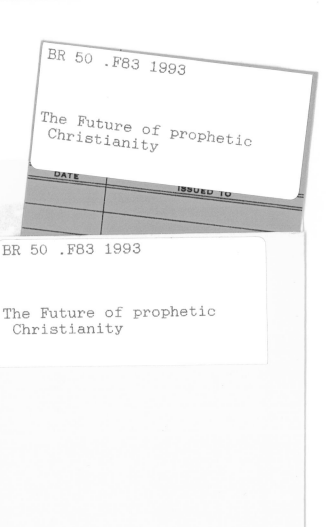

BR 50 .F83 1993

The Future of prophetic
Christianity

BR 50 .F83 1993

The Future of prophetic
Christianity

DATE   ISSUED TO

DEMCO